# WHAT'S WRONG WITH THE NATIONAL CURRICULUM ?

by Paul Francis

Published by Liberty Books
7, Swan Meadow, Much Wenlock, Shropshire  TF13 6JQ.

Copyright© 1992
Printed by Wozencroft Printers
ISBN 0 9520568 0 1

This book is dedicated

TO MY TEACHING COLLEAGUES

who remain

- despite the rhetoric -

responsible.




It is also in memory of

my father, David Francis (1904-92),

who would understand.

# Foreword

This is a highly topical book. Since I first finished it (in December 1991), it has been revised monthly, and publication - here more than ever - is an act of faith. There must be more to come, but you have to stop somewhere, and I think the basic case will remain.

# Acknowledgments

I would like to thank the following, for permission to quote extracts from their publications:
Daily Express;  Daily Mail;  Daily Mirror;  The Sun;
The Guardian;  The Observer;  Penguin Books.

Many teaching colleagues will recognise particular pages here. The observation of lessons, discussions in school and a range of chance contacts have contributed to this book.
There is no way of identifying all the debts, but it is my sense of a teaching community, committed, concerned, but above all honest, which makes me think there is a purpose in writing this.

My thanks are also due to Chris Cannon, for reading through the whole text, but particularly for putting me right about the impact of National Curriculum on primary schools. Any errors remain my own, but without him there would have been more. Colin Whitehead has been a patient and supportive computer guru, to whom I have frequently turned in times of word-processing trouble, and Mark Wozencroft who has done everything I have asked of Wozencroft Printers, at amazing speed.

I am also in debt to Linda, Ian and Hilary, who have tolerated my anti-social writing habits with wit and good humour, and been forgiving about the occasional embarrassments which my efforts have caused them.

Much Wenlock
December 1992

# WHAT'S WRONG WITH THE NATIONAL CURRICULUM ?

# Introduction: ROCKING THE BOAT

What's wrong with the National Curriculum ?

That sounds a bit negative, criticising at just the moment when our education system is on the mend. Things are getting better, we are told, not only by Government ministers but by the media. Each sign of incompetence, each source of anxiety, is rapidly picked on as one more demonstration of our national problem, soon to be solved by our National Curriculum. It is almost "in place", like some massive edifice being moved gradually into position. So what am I doing, as an unknown teacher, cynically picking holes ?

I'm not alone. I don't formally represent anyone, but I do work in a school and meet with other teachers, and I know that there are many people in education - parents, governors and advisers, as well as teachers - who agree with what much of what I have to say. And they do so more in sorrow and in anger. It is not that they want the National Curriculum to fail, or that they are against the whole idea, but what is currently proposed is not the best we can manage. It is not part of the solution, but part of the problem.

This view is rarely expressed. Instead, we are offered the myth of inevitable improvement, which acknowledges that there may be teething problems, but promises that ultimately we shall have an education system which delivers the goods. The good ship Quality has been sighted on the horizon, sailing steadily towards the harbour. All we have to do is wait patiently, and avoid rocking the boat.

But it's not true. To show why it's not true takes time, which is why this is a book rather than a pamphlet, but we have to start by saying that the myth is false. It suits politicians and the media to adopt a "common sence approach", to pretend that the whole business is very simple if only these waffly professionals wouldn't go around complicating things, but education is not simple. And if you want a demonstration of that, look at the mess that results when politicians turn their easy answers into law.

Take spelling, for example. This became ministerial obsession in 1991, was eventually imposed on the GCSE boards in 1992, and in September 1992 John Patten sought to exclude poor spellers from university. It is important to see the punitive nature of this interest; there is no intellectual concern (How is good spelling taught ? Will research show us if all pupils can become good spellers?), or even a capitalist incentive (rewards for good spellers, higher pay for the most successful teachers of good spelling). It is simply a question of penalising bad spelling.

In tabloid terms, this can be presented as a concern for academic standards. It sounds reasonable when Baroness Blatch says "We do a disservice to the school children of this country if we allow them to think sloppy written work is acceptable." But we have to think about it. Is all bad spelling sloppiness? Will simple effort cure it ? And does Baroness' Blatch's concern mean that teachers and examiners have hitherto accepted that sloppy written work is acceptable?

In August 1992, the first year in which exam boards were forced by the government to take special account of spelling, John Patten questioned the value of those results. He did not even raise the issue at a meeting with the exam boards, the week before the results came out. As soon as they were published, though, he issued a statement which said that marking was unreliable, and that the correction of spelling errors had not been carried out efficiently.

His source, ironically, was a report by HMI - whose "independent evidence" has not generally been welcomed by this government. This is what HMI actually said:
"The introduction of marks for spelling, punctuation and grammar appeared to have had an adverse effect on the validity of awarding decisions."
( HMI report on GCSE, 1992, section 23)

In other words, the government initiative has not only failed to produce an improvement in spelling; it has got in the way of the main business of the examination, and meant that the eventual results are less reliable than they would have been if the government had not intervened. But to know this you have to look far beyond the headlines, and spend the time and effort necessary to grasp the meaning of the small print.

There is a further reason why the National Curriculum has not been fully discussed. It is mainly the product, not of educational thinking, but of practical politics, and specifically the politics of the Thatcher government. Part of this involves a determination to push ahead, to ignore criticism and waste no time on consultation. And part of it involves the deliberate stifling of dissent, by reducing the independence of those best placed to question what is going on.

Thus employees of the National Curriculum Council must clear any public statement in advance. Teacher members of NC working groups are discouraged from discussing the deliberations of those groups, and prohibited from making any criticism of their findings. Chief Education Officers are conscious of their councillors, and head teachers of their governors. Her Majesty's Inspectors face extinction, but well before that threat their scope for public comment had been savagely reduced.

This pressure against public statement might be appropriate for the movement of Cruise missiles or the use of Government sweeteners in industry, but it makes a strange context for educational debate. It means that we have a curiously tame public discussion, from which many of the most expert voices have been excluded. The result may be apparent consensus, but that is not because the whole of education speaks with a single voice; it is because most of the voices have not been heard.

In his essay on Liberty, John Stuart Mill wrote:
"There is the greatest difference between presuming an opinion to be true, because, with every opportunity for contesting it, it has not been refuted, and assuming its truth for the purpose of not permitting its refutation. Complete liberty of contradicting and disproving our opinion, is the very condition which justifies us in assuming its truth for purposes of action; and on no other term scan a being with human faculties have any rational assurance of being right."

That is the liberty which we have lost, and the main purpose of this book is to reclaim it - to argue that our first loyalty is to the truth. When we speak the truth as we know it, then there is the chance that we may be right, or wrong, or partially misguided, but first we must be free to speak the truth.

At present, we have slogans, and slurs. We have a common, broadcast assumption that teachers are either misguided or incompetent or both, but that a government act will somehow improve the work done by their pupils. I think that assumption is nonsense, and I believe that a large number of parents, governors and councillors know it to be nonsense. It is also my belief that many of these people genuinely wish to understand education better, and want to play some active, intelligent part in its improvement. That is the faith on which this book depends, and while it could be dismissed as optimistic it is certainly not cynical.

It is not our fault. Professional educationists bear very little direct responsibility for development over the past five years. Our opinion has not been sought, and when expressed it has not been heeded. Government has taken upon itself not merely the power to oversee education, but the right to make frequent decisions regarding the details of its content and assessment. They did it their way, and the mess is theirs alone.

But it is our fault. We allowed large numbers of parents to be baffled by what we were doing with their children. We failed to come up with a clear, consistent pattern of assessment in which pupils and parents could have confidence. We never worked hard enough or cared sufficiently to create a body which could clearly articulate the views of the teaching profession. If only by default, we helped educate a public which was insufficiently critical to question the plausible promises of Quality and Choice. And most recently, we have failed to articulate to parents and to the public at large the serious, lasting damage being done to our work by Government reforms. None of these seemed like drastic crimes at the time, and they were mainly sins of omission, but we are paying for them now.

Since 1987 the teaching profession has been subjected to a series of ministerial assaults, some of them now admitted to be whimsical or due to election fever. The effect of this barrage has been twofold. First, it has put teachers under sustained pressure, sapping their ability to reflect on what is done, and to respond constructively to it. Second, the sheer volume of activity blunts our sense of history, so that by contrast with the hectic career of Kenneth Clarke, Kenneth Baker's role as Education Minister comes to seem positively statesmanlike. His Education Act, it is assumed, is part of the historic context within which we have to work.

Current rhetoric reinforces this illusion of progress. It speaks of reforms "working through", like benevolent medicine inexorably taking effect, but that is not how it feels from the inside. We are not in the middle of tough, bracing improvement; we are suffering damage, and the damage increases daily, aggravated by underfunding and a failure on the part of ministers and media to understand what is going on.

Two trivial, topical illustrations demonstrate the crisis. In September 1992 John Patten threw doubt on the whole validity of the GCSE assessment, implying that high grades were being awarded too freely, for work of inferior quality. The HMI report offered the consolation that things will improve when GCSE adopts the grading system of the National Curriculum:

"the more precise specification in the ATs has the potential to ensure better uniformity and continuity of examining standards in the future." (HMI report on GCSE, 1992, section 24)

I don't believe this, and I don't know of any teacher who does. The change in 1994 is simply cosmetic, from seven grades to ten. There is not time to change outline of syllabuses, design of papers or marking procedure; the main change is in how grades will be reported - from A-G to 1-10. And in one important respect, 1994 grades will be less precise than hitherto, because the new system will blur the C/D borderline. With consistent government encouragement on maintaining the "O-level equivalent", the line between grades C and D has always been a priority for exam boards, and a crude guide for colleges and employers. Yet in 1994 it will not be there. So why are these respectable voices assuring us that National Curriculum will solve the problems of assessment ?

In the same month, September 1992, "The Guardian" ran a series of adverts for its Education Guardian section. The picture showed a middle-aged teacher and surly pupil glumly staring into space, united in their disenchantment. "If you dread going back to school as much as your pupils...." it began, offering the reading of Education Guardian as the solution to this despair.

The larger print itemised some of the things depressing this weary pedagogue - "STRUGGLING WITH EXTRA HOMEWORK, SWEATING FOR EXAMS, COPING WITH CONTINUAL ASSESSMENT. IT'S NOT EASY BEING A TEACHER." In the small print you are assured that "Every Tuesday you'll find articles to help you plan your lessons around the National Curriculum."

What's interesting is that "continual assessment" is offered as a cause of depression, while "the National Curriculum" is just a fact of life, something around which you'll need to plan your lessons. Any realistic picture of an embittered teacher would surely include the pressures of the National Curriculum in the catalogue of reasons for despair, but a genteel convention precludes the possibility that there may be something wrong with the National Curriculum. It is at the demolition of this convention that this book is aimed.

In July 1992 John Patten, Minister of Education, published a White Paper which was intended to cement the Government's reforms for at least twenty-five years. According to the rhetoric, the flurry of activity was over, the last piece slotted into the jig-saw, and all that remained to be done was to consolidate the gains. How nice if that were true.

There is no reason why a series of rushed, secretive and unco-ordinated decisions should produce a lasting structure. In fact, the closer we look at what we have, and how it was put together, the less faith we can have in its ability to last. The original motive for the National Curriculum, the timescale of its creation, the manner of its definition and the underlying thinking - each of these suggest a limited, precarious future, and the process of disintegration has already begun.

Can we start again ? Are there alternatives ? It's a bleak prospect, either way, but the starting point - with Mill's encouragement - must be a clear, honest appraisal of what we have and what it means.

# CHAPTER ONE: Politics and Education

The relationship between politics and education in this country has always been difficult. The development of our system leaves us with a bewildering range of schools - from different religious denominations, founded by churches and by individuals, funded in a variety of ways. It is misleading to talk of a 'system' at all, and for years governments accepted that they would have little influence upon what went on in schools.

There was an acceptance that "this is the way things are", and occasionally controversy would break out - the 11 plus was challenged and replaced by comprehensive schools, Mr. Callaghan announced a Great Debate about education - but the impact on lessons was minimal.

Education was a low priority post in the cabinet, the place to put worthy politicians who deserved recognition but weren't actually going anywhere, and as a result few Education Secretaries did much to affect the work for which they were responsible.

One exception was Antony Crosland, the Labour Minister who did most to promote the spread of comprehensive schools. He was active and committed in pressing for this change, prepared to make demands and use the power of government to implement policy. He was, however, clear about the distinction between his work and that of the experts:
"I didn't regard either myself or my officials as in the slightest degree competent to interfere with the curriculum. We're educational politicians and administrators, not professional educationists."

For years that would have seemed a statement of the obvious, but not with the coming of Mrs. Thatcher. Professionals were suspect, in the civil service, the law and medicine, as well as in education. Professionals spoke their own confusing language, tried to patronise or deceive, and needed to be taken in hand. So Keith Joseph, as Mrs. Thatcher's close confidant and Education Secretary , was encouraged to clear away the clutter and sort the teachers out.

Unfortunately, he was also presiding over an education system which was seriously underfunded, in which the value of teachers' pay had fallen dramatically, and on which Government ministers made serious and regular attacks. This led to a direct confrontation between teachers and government which caused Joseph deep distress but which he was not equipped to resolve.

From 1983 to 1985 there was the "teachers' action", a sprawling, bad-tempered series of disputes, involving various measures on the part of teachers - strikes, working to rule, and "withdrawal of goodwill", whereby teachers suspended voluntary activities at lunchtime and after school. This was a bitter campaign which left damaging memories with parents and pupils, teachers and politicians.

For the Thatcher cabinet, it was the final, clear demonstration that education was in a mess and needed to be sorted out. Never again could they afford to allow teachers the freedom to disrupt education. Teachers' limited ability to negotiate their own pay was removed absolutely, and a minimal contract of commitments (Baker's "1265 hours") was drawn up and made legally binding. There were now some things which all teachers had to do, enforced by the power of the law.

From that it was a logical step to proceed to the actual business of education, to legislate about what should be taught. From the teachers' point of view, the National Curriculum was part of this process of clamping down, of government demonstrating its power over the teaching profession through the obvious means - legislation.

Fascinated with this new and powerful toy, secure in a large majority, it must have seemed the best way of establishing particular values and approaches. In fact, hasty legislation simply devalues the law in the eyes of those who must operate it, as well as providing odd moments of comic relief when the legislators change their minds and then have to repeal their own laws in order to clear themselves.

The history of the '44 act should have been a warning. A well-meant political and religious compromise has supposedly ensured that every school in the country has run an act of daily worship since 1944. But this has not happened, prosecutions are unheard of, and when anyone presumes to take the act seriously large numbers of people get embarrassed and look at the ceiling. In the same way, simply making National Curriculum the law of the land will not turn it into good education or an effective framework; it just adds to the anxieties of some teachers.

Not that National Curriculum was solely a political ploy. Other countries had some form of National Curriculum, and many educationists had independently been arguing for some form of common framework. As the National Curriculum developed, so it absorbed some educational ideas which were very different from the initial assumptions of Kenneth Baker.

## SECRETARIES OF STATE FOR EDUCATION

It may seem surprising to focus so brutally on personalities, to identify particular moves as belonging to Keith Joseph or Kenneth Baker. Surely education is a complex social process, more profound than the obsession with figureheads which so delights our media commentators ?

It should be, but the sad result of recent developments in education has been to personalise matters very closely around the individual who happens to be Secretary of State. (The clearest demonstration of this, as we shall see, is the brief career of John MacGregor). The Education Reform Act of 1988 was not the culmination of gradual developments, but the distinctive handiwork of Kenneth Baker, responding to the crisis which had engulfed his successor, and also demonstrating his powers of leadership to the prime minister.

It was therefore more important to get the legislation through than to ensure that it would work; more effective to crush teacher dissent than to respond to constructive criticism. These features also help to explain some of the problems with which we are still trying to cope. The Baker National Curriculum was constructed in haste, for political rather than educational motives, to demonstrate a public victory rather than to achieve a practical reform.

The inadequacy of Baker's National Curriculum is demonstrated by the problems he bequeathed to his successors. If NC really was a monolithic achievement of quality, subsequent education secretaries would simply inherit it, praise it and wait for the benefits to show. In fact they have had to scurry busily round making speedy and considerable amendments, some of which are themselves later amended.

Kenneth Baker left Education soon after the ERA legislation was passed, to take charge of the Conservative Party. (That he and many commentators should see this as a promotion was itself a gloomy sign of the times). The change of tone with John MacGregor's succession was instantaneous:
"In the short period I have been secretary of state many of you have impressed upon me that you warmly welcome the reforms but that you cannot do

everything at once. I am also sensitive and sympathetic to your pleas that overstraining that goodwill and commitment can endanger the very success of the reforms themselves. "

The emphasis was on making the thing workable, reducing demands, talking with professionals about how best to manage the change. This meant a more conciliatory tone, and substantial changes in the actual content of the curriculum. It also led to a clearer recognition in the documents of the active role of teachers, and their need to be involved in the process.

After Baker, this was a drastic change, although it was in effect a return to the old days, where politicians who knew that they were not experts also recognised that they would need the help and advice of people who were.

In the Thatcher cabinet, this was heresy. Sustained attacks were mounted on MacGregor, from Conservative Central Office and elsewhere, and one of Mrs. Thatcher's last acts as Prime Minister was to replace him with Kenneth Clarke.

There was a brief lull, a month or so to allow him to read the papers and find his feet. And then it started. Confident judgements on the content of History, Art and PE syllabuses, dismissive attacks on particular ways of teaching reading or assessing technical errors. The MacGregor revision of the National Curriculum became a wholesale slaughter, so radical that if a Labour Government had undertaken it they would be attacked as educational vandals. The Clarke National Curriculum totally overhauled the Baker version, launched with such glowing confidence a mere four years before. Yet because the same government was in power, and because the media were generally happy to broadcast their version of events, this retreat provoked little comment.

Hardly a month went by in which Kenneth Clarke did not pronounce on some fresh educational issue. It might be the use of coursework in assessment, the choice of books for schools or the quality of school inspection by HMI - all matters which you would think require considerable care and thought. Perhaps evidence might be produced, research quoted or detailed comparisons made with parallel situations elsewhere ? No. We became accustomed to bluff statements that x was common sense, y was barmy and z daft, and that was all there was to it.

This is assertion, crude and simple, and if he didn't win the arguments he changed the rules - or the players. SEAC was set up to do the government's bidding on assessment; when the experience of the members of SEAC led them towards conclusions unacceptable to the government, they were sacked and Lord Griffiths, chairman of the Centre for Policy Studies, was brought in.

We have lost the distinction between serving party and serving the country. Kenneth Clarke had no sense of setting up a pattern to command national support, beyond this government or after an election. He was using power while he had it, regardless of the long-term cost. What would he expect a future Labour government to do - sack the head of SEAC and bring in their own extremist ? And if so, how could teachers have any lasting confidence in the work of either?

This was the logical extension of the Thatcher inheritance, which prefers action to talk, and despises consultation as a waste of time. There is a heady excitement about this pattern, a sense of "getting things done" which can sometimes obscure an older, wiser tradition:

"The whole strength and value, then, of human judgement,depending on the one property, that it can be set right when it is wrong, reliance can be placed on it only when the means of setting it right are kept constantly at hand. In the case of any person whose judgement is really deserving of confidence, how has it become so ? Because he has kept his mind open to criticism of his opinions and conduct. Because it has been his practice to listen to all that could be said against him. No wise man ever acquired his wisdom in any mode but this; nor is it in the nature of human intellect to become wise in any other manner."

That, J.S. Mill reminds us, is the test. How would he know, how would we know, if Kenneth Clarke were wrong ? It would be no better if he were a Labour minister, or a lifelong student of educational theory. No one person should be in a position of such power, free to operate in defiance of the views of others.

This point is forcefully made by Cox and Marks, at the conclusion of "The Insolence of Office" (The Claridge Press, 1988) —
"It is not only that the educational establishment has shown that it cannot be trusted. The truth is that no educational establishment - or any other establishment holding power - is to be trusted. This was well put by Edmund Burke, more than 200 years ago:
'In my course I have known and, according to my measure, have co-operated with great men; and I have never yet seen any plan which has not been mended by the observations of those who were much inferior in understanding to

the person who took the lead in the business'" (pp67-8)

Kenneth Clarke was the extreme version of ministerial intervention, more concerned with impact and image than with work in schools. The "Three Wise Men" report was issued to the press two weeks before it reached the heads of primary schools. Journalists were given complex documents minutes before a press conference, while brief league tables would be issued well in advance. As Clarke pointed out "It makes the questioning so much easier".

For education, this was an eventful, damaging reign, but Kenneth Clarke's departure did not solve the problem. He left behind him a series of arbitrary and destructive decisions, and helped to blur the deeper problems raised by the National Curriculum: what do we want all pupils to know ? what should they be able to do ? how can parents most clearly understand the progress children have made ?

There is no logical connection between  National Curriculum  and a dictatorial style of government. It is, in fact, a heady, liberating exercise to imagine a national curriculum without the restless, contemptuous management which has generally overseen its introduction. It is accident that our current NC has coincided with a period of frantic ministerial intervention, but only when we have a curriculum which is independent of political fashion can we expect to build any serious foundations for the future.

This is not to call for the return of ignorant or impotent ministers. Nor is it to argue for an alternative dictatorship, by educational professionals. There is a lot to be said for healthy scepticism, for questioning what experts say. But there is such a thing as experience, there are people who have expertise, and for politicians to assume that nobody in education can tell them anything they do not already know is a dangerous way to proceed. It is, in a word, ignorant.

# CHAPTER TWO: Education in the Media

Education has moved up the agenda. We are now more likely to find articles in newspapers and programmes on television which deal with work in schools, and that is good news. The purpose of this chapter is to look at how that is handled, at the filtering that goes on as the media deal with education in general, and the NC in particular.

From the start, you had to be careful. Angela Rumbold, minister of state at the DES, announced that "Of 11,790 representations, only 1,536 were opposed in principle." It sounds impressive, and it's one of the bricks on which the government has built an illusion of consensus.

But you need to look at the small print. The government did not invite comments on the principle of a National Curriculum. They provided a particular model, and neither the time allowed nor subsequent action suggested that they had been very responsive to the replies they received. Kenneth Baker was invited to publish the representations, but declined to do so; they were analysed by Julian Haviland, who wrote a book about them, and offered the estimate that 98% of responses were critical in some way. ("Take Care, Mr. Baker", published by Fourth Estate).

That's not the way it sounds when Angela Rumbold is quoted, and asking those sort of questions is precisely the job of an independent press. In this area, complicated and confusing as it is, journalists of all kinds have found it hard to maintain that independence, and have often settled for simplified versions in the same way as the politicians; often, in fact, it is the politicians' caricature which is simply transmitted to the viewer or reader.

This chapter deals with a few examples from December 1991. It is not suggested that this is a wide or representative sample (and there have certainly been better television programmes than "Class Wars"), but even in this brief selection there are recurrent features which are both disturbing and important.

TELEVISION:

Panorama - Class Wars.

The snappy, punning title should have been a warning. This programme was ostensibly about teaching methods, but it was also about a war - two sides in the educational debate, trendy against traditional. As teachers keep saying, in classroom operation it is not as simple as that, but hardly anybody listens.

This programme tried to cover a lot of ground - styles of teaching, degrees of informality, testing and the National Curriculum, teacher training, the place of classics in literature. They also had a spread of viewpoints - teachers to represent extremes of the teaching style spectrum, Ted Wragg (trendy), Roger Scruton and Iris Murdoch (traditional), and a couple of trainee student teachers.

This is where the programme became nasty. The college involved had declined to be filmed - and it is a sad reflection on previous programmes that many educational institutions now feel that "no comment" is the only safe response. Instead, the programme settled for a detailed interview with two education students. They were not representative in any obvious sense, and in retrospect it is hard to see why their views were given such prominence. They were encouraged to spell out their uncertainties and confusion, unwittingly illustrating a predetermined thesis that "teachers don't know what they're doing".

The result was depressing, and no doubt deeply worrying to parents - particularly if they felt that this was "the best we can do." Little was offered in the way of positive solutions for the future, although Roger Scruton was allowed to offer unchallenged the suggestion that all teacher training institutions should simply be closed down. It was a bad, muddled programme, which fed off and accentuated real concerns, without illuminating them in any way.


RADIO

The World at One: Interview with Kenneth Clarke.
(Radio Four, 14.12.91)

In this long interview, Kenneth Clarke was questioned about a range of educational issues, and invited to respond not only to questions, but also to taped comments from spokesmen for the Labour and Liberal Democrat parties, as well as from Peter Sullivan, a junior school head from Reading.

I had hoped to include detailed extracts from the interview, and to that end wrote to the three people involved . Nick Clarke (the interviewer) and Peter Sullivan were happy that I should use quotations from the programme, but I was unable to obtain Kenneth Clarke's permission before the book went to press. His comments are therefore paraphrased.

Peter Sullivan vividly described the impact on the education profession of ministerial disparagement:
"I think it's very disheartening for teachers, who are working very hard taking on board these changes, to go home, to listen to news broadcasts, to watch TV news and see people like Kenneth Clarke constantly criticising the teaching profession. I think it's most unfortunate, it's totally unnecessary and I think it's counter-productive. I think the secretary of state could achieve far more for the education service if he actually said 'Look, let's do this together, rather than simply trying to score political points.' "

Mr. Clarke's response to this damning charge was that he had never criticised teachers. He then claimed to have identified a public wish to see standards raised in schools, implying that such a desire was not there before. Were there no people working in education who also wished to raise standards ? For a man who never criticises teachers this was verging on the tactless.

One obstacle might be money. Mr. Sullivan described the working of his school's budget, the expenditure on staff salaries and running costs, and the fact that this left the equivalent of the price of a Mars bar each day to provide all the learning materials and resources for each child in his school. The secretary of state dismissed suggestions that schools were dependent on the £55 million pounds which parents annually donate to primary schools, implying that any school which did not have sufficient funds was not being properly managed.

The conversation moved on to the proposal to reduce the number of HMI, and to recruit outside bodies to inspect schools. The interviewer referred to the new inspection teams as "privatised companies." Kenneth Clarke took exception to this, but then moved into gratuitous insult - slandering the calibre of LEA inspectors and advisers. (It is interesting, but not surprising, to see that in practice most of the new inspectors will be educational professionals, and that the sweeping promise of change will not in fact be realised - yet again).

Through the interview, it is noticeable that Kenneth Clarke's preference is for combat, hitting the opposition rather than solving the problem. He is not alone among politicians in this, but it does make for distortion. He is unperturbed, for instance, by the considerable opposition to his proposals for inspection. He ridicules Jack Straw and "some of the more nervous members of the educational establishment", suggesting that their reluctance to approve the proposals stems from a fear of the truth. Their opposition, he implies, is simply a defensive reaction to the prospect of losing power.

We are a long, long way from John Stuart Mill. ("He who knows only his own side of the case knows little of that."). One of the "more nervous people in the educational establishment" is Eric Bolton, former Chief Inspector of Schools. Can his description of this move as a "minor but important tragedy" really be waved away so airily ?

HMI, Bolton argues, "has given sensible and broadly correct advice about the direction of national policy. All that seems to me to be at risk, almost thoughtlessly, without debate...Policy making will be less well-informed and short-sighted than it has been. It is a sad backward step and I cannot see why it needs to happen."

Is that really nervous terror about opening up the system ? It sounds to me like a rational expression of justified anxiety. And it is also a precise description of the process described by Mill, whereby an independent view tells us something we did not already know ("..because he has kept his mind open to criticisms of his opinions and conduct.").

The interviewer returned to the question of haste. Wasn't too much being done too fast ?

Clarke responded that his changes were based not only on the anxieties of the public, but on a substantial amount of research. Having perceived shortcomings in the pattern of education, he argued that he was obliged to provide the remedy. It was as simple as that. Parents wanted an immediate improvement in the quality of their children's education, not a future promise. He then went on to ridicule the approach of the Labour Party and the teaching unions, who in his view were simply postponing action, reluctant to make the necessary, urgent changes.

There are a lot of worrying things here.

(1) It is a precise example of Mr. Sullivan's criticism earlier in the interview - point-scoring rather than constructive partnership.

(2) It implies a simple process which in fact Government ministers have found it very difficult to carry out; if the remedies are so simple, why was Mr. Baker's definition of what school-leavers require so different from Mr. Clarke's ?

(3) Just what is the substantial research which has identified the weaknesses in English education ? It would help to have the sources named, and exposed to the scrutiny of public debate, but Mr. Clarke is uncharacteristically coy about his intellectual sources.

Mr. Sullivan was anxious that Mr. Clarke should develop a more sophisticated view of teachers at work:
"The Secretary of State is beginning to talk about traditional versus modern or progressive methods, and I think that's a false dichotomy." In his school, Mr. Clarke would see the same teacher using both traditional and modern methods within half an hour of each other.

Mr. Clarke was not convinced. Accepting such complications would blur the edges of debate, and he was happier with the clear, strong lines of caricature. He accused teachers of being influenced by strange ideas about education. This led, he argued, to a reluctance to actually instruct, a failure to correct mistakes or to set demanding tasks. Such teachers, Clarke suggested, were so disturbed by the prospect of a blackboard and orderly lines of chairs that in reaction they allowed their classrooms to turn into a cheerful kind of mayhem.

But who exactly did this ? When asked, Mr. Clarke says his target is educationists, the dotty ones with cranky theories. But his criticism is of work in schools, and if his picture is right then this is fundamentally a criticism of teachers. And if significant numbers of teachers have really been doing this, they should not continue to teach.
And what will be put in their place ? What primarily is Kenneth Clarke after ? In his final contribution, he listed the ideals he regarded as important - making demands on the brightest pupils in science and maths, as well as retaining A levels while supplementing them with equivalent technical qualifications. He wanted all children to fulfil their potential in various ways, taking account of individual differences.

So do we all. And if he had started there, and proceeded to develop that theme, showing exactly how provision might match the variations in pupil need, this would have been a different and a better interview. But squeezed in as a postscript, a final soundbite, to beat the approaching guillotine, there's not time to develop the idea. It's a politician's last word, not an educationist's programme.

This wasn't a bad interview. A lot of work and preparation had gone into it, and on both sides it was a pleasant, good-tempered and fluent exchange, which is not always the case. It followed a clear and orderly agenda, although there were times when Mr. Clarke simplified issues and evaded questions.

Most interviews are much less long and careful than this one, and the alert listener could learn something about government policy and teacher attitudes. I have had the benefit of hindsight and a transcript, and this allows a degree of critical attention which would normally be a luxury. It does show, though, the difficulty of focussing seriously on complex educational issues when a politician is more anxious to transmit a narrower, more specific message.

NEWSPAPERS

This is a brief comparison of how four popular newspapers covered the publication of the tests for 7-year olds, carried out in the summer of 1991 (and published on December 1991).

DAILY EXPRESS

The DAILY EXPRESS devoted most of pages 7 and 8 to the story. Page 7 gave two short tables, of "The top ten authorities" and "The worst 10 authorities", with a headline that read "PARENTS TO TEST SCHOOLS. 'Check out your local results', says Clarke."

Factual report was swiftly followed by analysis, although it was not made clear precisely who was doing the analysing:
"The Department of Education yesterday released figures showing overall attainment in the tests so far.
And trendy teaching methods were blamed for dramatic differences in the performance of seven year olds across Britain."

The DES released the figures, but Kenneth Clarke did the blaming. Much was made of the contrast between Richmond and Bradford (respectively top and bottom of the national league table), although a wider point was made but not followed up - "There were also widespread differences among education authorities within the same regions of the country."

A third of page 7 was devoted to a photograph and article about The Russell School, Richmond, which has a "friendly, relaxed atmosphere", dedicated staff and strong parental support. "The school uses both traditional teaching for the three Rs and less conventional methods."

Page 8, however, returned to a familiar theme "The bitter harvest of trendy teaching." It quotes a range of sources, but a limited range - Kenneth Clarke, Tory MP George Walden and Dr. Sheila Lawlor of the Centre for Policy Studies.

There was also a quarter-page article on Bradford, bottom of the league, where "many pupils...have to be taught English as a second language, teachers admitted last night." (Why should they have to admit that ? Are they guilty about it ? Isn't it true ?)

Teachers testified to high morale, their use of varied methods, and the fact that "The tests have not been fair in many cases, because they try to treat all children alike whereas there are many social and cultural differences."

The Education chairman argued that the tests were invalid, because other authorities had applied less stringent standards of assessment than Bradford.

DAILY MAIL

The DAILY MAIL offered two pages, with a headline running across both "AREA BY AREA, THE TEST RESULTS THAT REVEAL HOW MANY PRIMARY SCHOOLS ARE FAILING OUR YOUNGSTERS".

The article by the paper's education correspondent is headed "Teaching methods to blame as 30pc of pupils fail to make the grade." There is analysis of geographical and financial variations, and a confident quote from Kenneth Clarke:
"We now have solid evidence that, in the crucial early years, pupils are not making consistent progress across the full curriculum in the core subjects of English, mathematics and science.... Eventually I intend to publish seven-year-old results school by school. "

(Back in 1989, "From Policy to Practice" had promised "LEAs will not be required to publish 'league tables' for the schools in their area." (7.4) Times have changed).

The article quoted Bradford's education chairman - "a council can decide where it wants to end up in the tables by deciding how to mark the tests" - and was not impressed by the response from the profession. "Reaction from teachers leaders was either moaning or hostile."

Page 15 was filled with coverage of the test results, and two-thirds of that space went on a league table of scores, with 105 education authorities ranked under five headings -

OVERALL      (percentages at level 2 and above, and at level 3)
ENGLISH      (      "      )
MATHS        (      "      )
SCIENCE      (      "      )

SPENDING PER PUPIL

The rest of the page is divided into two. THE BEST describes Holy Trinity School in Richmond, where the council is keen on education, teachers work very hard and parents are very supportive. The education chairman says "We use a combination of traditional and progressive teaching methods and this combination  seems to have worked."

THE WORST describes Bradford, where the director of education says "Our schools adopt a wide range of techniques geared to a child's specific needs. They range from the traditional to self-discovery." She also argued that the figures did not compare like with like, since the marking of the tests was not standardised. A head teacher said that he was confident that teachers were doing a good job, while a parent found the results worrying, and felt the basics were not given the proper emphasis.

DAILY MIRROR

The DAILY MIRROR covered half of page 17, under a bold headline MUST DO BETTER. They gave a simplified table, listing all the authorities, but giving only three figures -
(1) Pupils average or bright
(2) Pupils who can't read or write properly
(3) Pupils who can't do sums.

The main comment on this was "Tests 'sham'" - "This was condemned as a SHAM by teachers and school chiefs last night." Bradford's problems with school buildings and large proportion of non-English speaking pupils were mentioned, while "Top rating goes to the leafy London suburb of Richmond where, by contrast, well-off parents can raise big money for education."

## THE SUN

The SUN devoted a tenth of page 4 to the story, exactly the same amount as it devoted to Terry Waite's attendance at a junior school nativity play. The headline was ONE IN FOUR PUPILS CAN'T ADD UP AT 7. It gave the following factual information:
"At least 28 per cent are unable to read without help. One in five cannot write and 27 per cent cannot count to 100 or add four to five."

These were referred to as "shock results", and Kenneth Clarke was quoted as saying that they highlighted "room for improvement", and justified his campaign to restore traditional teaching methods. Labour agreed that the figures were shocking, and condemned the Government for failing to raise standards.

For those who believe that the publication of results will raise the standard of debate, these papers make depressing reading. There is a delight in gloom and blame, a passionate curiosity in the extremes of any spectrum (Richmond and Bradford, forget what's in between), and a reluctance to get involved in serious issues which is very worrying.

Standardisation, for instance. It sounds boring and technical, but if it has not happened it makes a difference - especially if you live in Bradford. There was no work done to make sure that the marking of the tests was being carried out in the same way in different parts of the country; it would have taken longer, and it would have cost money (because teachers marking the tests have to be able to meet, to compare their marking) but it would have strengthened the claim that this is hard, objective information.

There were reservations about the actual method of testing. The British Psychological Society described it as an "elastic ruler" - but such criticisms were not mentioned in these articles (unless you count the MIRROR's wholesale allegation of a sham).

The actual use of the figures is very limited. The SUN did not print them at all, and the MIRROR's simplified version is dangerously misleading. There is also a tricky statistical point; what should the figures be ? Should everyone have achieved level 2 ? (Not if it's an average). Kenneth Clarke's claim that we now have "solid evidence" that pupils are not making "consistent progress" is untrue, unless "consistent progress" means "everyone proceeding at exactly the same rate in every subject." We could only measure progress if we had some starting point, an indication of pupils' achievement at the age of 5, and so far nobody has proposed testing there. These figures might give us a basis for measuring subsequent achievement, when these children are 11, but that is a different matter.

As it is, "testing at 7" is not a fair basis for comparison. "From Policy to Practice" said that "Schools will not be required to publish in their prospectuses aggregate results for 7 year olds, whose achievements will be strongly influenced by their length of time in school and pre-school experience, as well as their school progress." Because some pupils start in September, and some in the term in which they become five, "pupils aged seven" will include some who have spent two terms longer in school than others - almost twice as much. Those who started school in the autumn did better, and so on. But if the Government's own publicity made this clear in 1989, how could they have forgotten it two years later?

The blackest feature of these newspaper reports is the quality of the analysis. Many of these articles could have been written regardless of the test results - they are simply opinion, tacked on to the issue of the figures. Headlines broadcast their condemnation of trendy teaching methods, despite the fact that there is no evidence for this. All the teachers cited, at both ends of the results spectrum, went out of their way to insist that they made use of a variety of methods. There was no information available on the teaching methods employed to achieve any of these test results, and yet papers insist on making this analysis.

And not only papers. There was an unhealthy link between the tabloid papers and Kenneth Clarke, who confidently asserted that a quarter of the nation's seven-year olds were unable to read more than three letters of the alphabet. (The correct figure is less than 2 %). He later conceded that his information was drawn from a popular newspaper.

Reading tabloids is not a crime, but the Secretary of State does - or at least, should - have access to more reliable information. In this case, SEAC had received two evaluations of the tests two weeks before Mr. Clarke produced the results, in December 1991. Mr. Clarke said that neither socio-economic factors nor variations between teachers' assessments were important; both evaluations said they were crucial. Had Mr. Clarke read the evaluations, and decided to ignore them ? Or had he never received them ? This significant discrepancy was only revealed in the following April,when the author of one of the reports, Dr.

Diane Shorrocks, said "We are glad that the issue has been kept before the public. We were sworn to secrecy and had to tell people we could not divulge the details." (The Guardian, 7.4.92)

It sounds like Spycatcher. With an effort, we have to remember that all this is about seven year olds, and how they are doing in school. This, you would have thought, is information of interest to the public, something they have a right to know - not a dirty little secret to be suppressed. In the absence of reliable information and expert analysis, we are left with the amateurs. This is part of the MAIL's editorial:

"Intriguingly, some of the highest-spending authorities have some of the worst test results. It is quite possible that large classes actually yield better results because they are not suitable for applying trendy teaching methods."

Is it ? Does anyone seriously suppose that we shall get better quality education with fewer teachers and larger classes ? This is not constructive or responsible journalism, but it is prejudice sanctioned by government. The sloppy thinking, the contempt for evidence, the relish with which professionals are attacked are all echoes of government ministers in action.

For a more positive approach we can turn, perhaps with surprise but also some relief, to the editorial in the SUN:
"It's too easy simply to blame lack of money or trendy teachers. Learning should start at home. Tonight, switch off the TV and get out a book. Read it with your children. Stretch their minds. Education is too important to be left to schools."

# CHAPTER THREE: Curriculum for What ?

## THE IDEA OF A NATIONAL CURRICULUM

The notion is attractive. For years the English educational system has been varied but chaotic, tackling different subjects in different ways, with no guarantee of a common minimum across the land.

A National Curriculum seems to offer stability and reassurance, guaranteeing consistency to all - pupils and parents as well as teachers. That is why the idea is so appealing, and that is partly why it has been welcomed by people outside education. Politicians find it difficult to openly attack something that seems so sensible. Well, of course we should all know where we are...

But where are we ? As the Education Reform Bill was drawn up, turned into an Act, implemented and then subsequently refined, the precise purpose of the National Curriculum has changed, so that now it is  not precise at all. In various ways, and at various times, different people expect the National Curriculum to achieve the following aims:
- provide a broad and balanced education for all pupils
- guarantee parents a quality education for their children
- prepare pupils better for the world of work
- enable us to compete economically with other countries
- raise the basic standards of literacy
- give each pupil a clear idea of future targets.

Each of these may be admirable, but they are not the same, and it would be a very flexible piece of legislation which guaranteed to implement them all.

Take standards of literacy, for instance. It would be reasonable to see this as a priority, to devote resources to ensuring that no pupil left junior school without being able to read and write at a certain minimum level of competence. The Reading Recovery Programme, pioneered in New Zealand, is one way of achieving this, and has an impressive record for winning over sceptics. But it involves 1:1 teaching ratios some of the time, a lot of training and careful monitoring of progress - in other words, money. You only do this if you think it matters, and if you clearly make it a priority.

Personally, if I had to make an unreal choice between the National Curriculum and Reading Recovery, I would go for the latter every time. It is based on detailed observation of professionals at work; it is free of dogma, in the practical sense that it makes use of a variety of methods, without exalting one above all others; and it has been systematically evaluated, not only by those responsible for running it, but by sceptical observers who have then become convinced. As a result it has been adopted in Australia, different parts of America, and Surrey, and with pupils from an impressive range of backgrounds. Mill would have loved it.

Yet we shall only be doing this in a small number of schools, and the teachers being asked to oversee this progress in reading will simultaneously be asked to master new, complex demands in technology and science, as well as maintaining their present responsibility for English, Maths, History, Geography, Art, Music and PE. John Patten declined to appear on a television programme on Reading Recovery (8.9.92), but justified the small scale of investment with the suggestion that this was "a pilot".

This is ludicrous. What else in our current education system is being "piloted", in the sense that a limited trial run is then subject to sustained professional scrutiny and open debate ? Ministerial arrogance has replaced the traditional use of hypothesis, evidence and analysis, and in any case an interested sceptic can consult an impressive body of international work which already testifies to the superiority of Reading Recovery over other programmes, including other programmes which make use of 1:1 teaching. It's been done; all they have to do is read it, and decide how much they are prepared to spend. The answer is, not a lot.

The basic question remains: is there a priority, or not ? Being a primary teacher must involve versatility, the simultaneous pursuit of different aims, but to achieve some measurable success there has to be a clear direction, and a reasonable timescale in which to get there. With National Curriculum, there are conflicting and simultaneous demands, and unreal expectations which are constantly revised.

In secondary schools, National Curriculum outlines an impressive array of cross-curricular themes, dimensions and skills which schools should be aware of and promote. It is hard to believe that this was a central part of Kenneth Baker's intention, but somebody (probably HMI) ensured that cross-curricular aspects were included. If NC says what is important, then anything omitted from NC is seen to be trivial. So these issues were added, and rightly - but teachers are not in a position to do anything about them at precisely the time when demands on them as <u>subject teachers</u> have never been higher.

For the NC to work, we need a more honest estimate of its aims. Consistency, for example. One justification for a National Curriculum is the way in which pupils who move between schools are at the mercy of diverse syllabuses and practices. A child moving from Kent to Cumberland may never study the Romans at all; alternatively, they may study the Romans in Kent, and then discover twelve months later that they are due to study the Romans in Cumberland.

What is the solution to this problem ? NC can decide that study of the Romans is a prerequisite for an educated child, that all pupils approaching KS 3 shall attend some lessons about the Romans. Fine. But to avoid the Kent/Cumberland problem you have to stipulate that all lessons on the Romans should take place at precisely the same time - otherwise the risks of duplication or omission will remain.

We have until recently prided ourselves on the independence of our education system, and laughed at caricatures of the French pattern, in which the Education Minister consults his diary and says "Ah, le quatorze janvier. Today we study the semi-colon."

But it's not a joke. Either you control things that tightly, or you accept the risks. Just how prescriptive do we mean to be, and what is the degree of freedom left to individual teachers ?

And what exactly is being prescribed ? Much of the NC rhetoric is about quality, good learning, but when you study the actual detail it is mainly concerned with content. Pupils must cover the Romans, knowledge about language, calculation and so on, and that is what is prescribed. What's good about studying the Romans, or how pupils will benefit from that, is left undefined.

There are pious phrases about flexibility, but if this operation were anxious to give teachers real freedom then all the syllabuses would be a lot shorter. If you want a workable framework for teachers, or a clear outline of priorities, then you take the tough decisions and leave something out. As it is, the sheer bulk of this elastic monster is beyond most people's comprehension.

SUBJECTS

What is the NC ? The simple answer is subjects. NC definitions are mainly concerned with subject headings, English and Maths, Science,

30

Technology and so on. This is not surprising, in the sense that our secondary schools and examination system have always been dominated by subjects, but there are still problems with the method.

First of all, the extent to which primary schools teach subjects varies considerably. This topic is widely discussed within junior schools, and much advice has been directed towards them (usually by secondary specialists) to adopt a more subject-centred approach.

That they have not universally done so is not the result of simple cussedness. Small schools cannot afford specialists; each teacher has to be versatile, working across a range of subjects - a range substantially increased by National Curriculum. So that while many may have particular strengths and enthusiasms, it is not possible for them to spend their entire teaching time on these.

And it may not be desirable. Subject specialists means pupil movement between teachers, and while there may be limitations in the "single class teacher" model there are also serious problems involved in rapid transition between rooms and teachers. Some schools and some teachers choose not to divide their work into subjects because to do so would make arid distinctions. If the English teacher does all the English work, and the Maths teacher does all the Maths work, then nobody sees Serena do her English and her Maths work, and it is as important to know about Serena (as a learner in English, and as a learner in Maths) as it is to know about English, or about Maths.

There are also positive benefits from combining work in various subject disciplines on a common theme. Take windmills. I recently visited one junior school where a class were spending a term on windmills. Not every piece of work in the term related to windmills, but they did visit windmills, write about them, look at pictures of them, draw and paint them, construct their own windmills, test and evaluate them in action, and so on. In terms of subjects, the work would be recognised and valued by teachers of English, Art, Maths, Drama, Science and Technology (at least), but I can see no advantage in precisely allocating short areas of time to each of these activities, or in ensuring that pupils are aware of the difference between Science work on windmills and Technology work on windmills.

This was a lively class responding to a teacher's interest in windmills. Nobody is saying that everyone has to do windmills for a term, but if we do have a National Curriculum then it should be one which allowed such work to continue, rather than encouraging teachers to subdivide what they and their pupils do into predetermined snippets.

NC insists that learning is to be defined in terms of subjects - and that junior schools now need to organise and record what they do in that form. In December 1991 Kenneth Clarke demanded that junior schools should change their teaching pattern so as to suit the NC better, and he set up a working party to come to this conclusion. The timescale was tight, the evidence limited and no practising primary teachers were involved, but the overall sequence is very strange:
(1) Define a National Curriculum
(2) Instruct schools to change their approach
(3) Look - briefly - at the evidence.
Surely it would make more sense to look first at the work going on in schools, then define a National Curriculum, and only then to consider any changes in method which might be necessary.

THE SECONDARY CURRICULUM

The NC pattern ought to be more attractive to secondary schools, since it appears to favour them. In the early days, there was a brief strand of optimism which implied that the NC would act as a boost to curricular innovation:
"In due course, it is likely that schools will 'throw all the attainment targets in a heap on the floor and reassemble them in a way which provides for them the very basis of a whole curriculum.'" (The Whole Curriculum, NCC 3 p.1)

This is a bad joke. Even the revised, slimmed-down attainment targets make a massive collection, and I see no sign of staff wanting to redefine the subject boundaries. Many would be happy for someone else to relieve them of the excessive workload NC imposes on them, but few are actually looking for more work (let alone the colossal effort involved in Geography, say, testing some of the mathematical attainment targets and keeping Mathematics teachers informed of the progress of various pupils.)

So it's business as usual, but with one crucial, damaging difference. Most secondary schools have a senior teacher responsible for timetabling. They first draw up a curriculum plan, which shows how each class in the school will spend each week in the school year - five lessons for English, or four for Maths. This is worked out, and set against the teacher periods available; these are the Art lessons we plan to teach next year - do they match the teaching time which teachers of Art have available ?

This is an obvious precaution, to make sure that the whole thing fits, before drawing up an actual timetable of which lessons will be taught on which days. But the amazing fact about the NC for secondary schools was that this elementary calculation was never carried out. Working groups were set up for a wide range of subjects, without any of them knowing how much time was available.

The result was predictable. Any group of enthusiasts, people who care about a subject and want its importance recognised, will press for the maximum - this theme must be done, this skill is essential, this topic is necessary as a preliminary to....and so on. If you have a lot of content, you need a lot of time, and you need a lot of teachers to teach it. Among other things, the NC was a power auction, in which subject bids made claims for importance within the curriculum as a whole. Time, teachers and resources are the currency of schools, and it is in the allocation of these things that priorities are defined. But in a school there is someone at the centre, with both knowledge and control, to say "No. I'm sorry, it's a good idea, but there simply isn't time."

There was no such person to control the NC. Like Topsy, it growed and growed. In the early days, it was common to hear school timetablers talk of "using 120% of the time available ". Humble protestations that "The National Curriculum is not the whole curriculum" cut little ice with staff who could not find the necessary time to teach the National Curriculum, let alone anything that might exist outside it.

It would have helped to have some guidelines, indications of how many lessons should be allocated to each subject, but all we got were coy references to "a reasonable amount of time." In years 10 and 11 (which used to be fourth and fifth years), GCSE subjects usually get a minimum of two double lessons a week - 10% . So, if English, Maths, Two Sciences, Technology, Languages, History, Geography, Art and  Music were all to get their fair share, that was the time accounted for.

No P.E., though, or Personal and Social Education. If school pupils had to be told about AIDS, where was that going to go ? And what about the possibilities for specialisation which always used to be on offer - classics, two foreign languages or business studies ? Or possible vocational courses like office practice, catering or motor vehicle maintenance ?

These are tricky questions, but every secondary school answers them before they write their timetable. Sometimes it involves hard choices, like shutting down courses because there aren't enough takers, or closing down a good educational opportunity because the staffing isn't available. With the National Curriculum there was no senior teacher responsible, no timetabler with the nerve or power to say it didn't fit.

Mr. Baker had his own timetable, which involved a public demonstration of power as soon as possible. Although the necessary thinking had not been done, the Act was passed, the television appearances took place and thousands of glossy booklets were produced.

REVISION AND RETREAT

"From Policy to Practice" now makes salutary reading. One of the first and most extravagant of a series of National Curriculum publications, its fifty pages ooze with authority - wide margins, generous spacing, good quality paper. A series of sections and subsections, from 1.1 to 11.1, with five annexes and a list of further reading. What more could you ask ?

One thing you could ask for is permanence. Four years later it is all out of date. The confident definition announces that "The National Curriculum comprises three core subjects and seven other foundation subjects which must be included in the curricula of all pupils." (3.3)   But now they don't.

Nobody is very confident about how Technology should be defined, but if it's really to be studied by all pupils throughout the school then it can't be too technical (expensive on equipment), and it must have a fairly flexible definition or there won't be sufficient staff to go round. In  most junior schools it is a new subject, creating considerable unease among those required to teach it, and its assessment at all levels remains problematic.

Languages for all was a fine ideal, but they hadn't taken the preliminary step of checking that there were enough language teachers around to put it into practice (let alone deciding which language or languages were to be taught, and how it was going to be possible to teach anyone two languages if the National Curriculum only allowed room for one).

After a brief flirtation with short courses, History and Geography are now to be alternatives higher up the school, as will Art and Music. PE can expect some kind of future life but only if it is understood in a more "flexible" sense, whatever that means. (Gymnastics for all, perhaps ?) So what we can be sure of is that all pupils from 11 - 16 will be doing English, Maths and Science - but most of them were, anyway.

In 1991 Kenneth Clarke envisaged a wider spread of "options", pupils choosing from a range of courses, rather than being required to follow compulsory courses. "Choice" is a possible value, but it is totally opposed to the "broad and balanced" model which Kenneth Baker originally proposed - "three core subjects and seven foundation subjects which must be included in the curricula of all pupils. " Not much choice there. Within four hectic and expensive years, the fundamental definition of the National Curriculum has been changed, and that is bound to undermine the confidence with which the project can be viewed.

For teachers, it is galling to have to keep revising plans, to throw away good work because it is no longer required, to postpone planning decisions because the government has not yet made up its mind - or has changed its mind again. Much teacher time has been squandered, in planning meetings, wasted effort and the determined assimilation of boring regulations which are rapidly superseded by revised boring regulations. Primary teachers were encouraged to develop fiercely detailed record-keeping systems, which were subsequently altered or scrapped. Much government money has been wasted on printing glossy booklets reporting on the progress of the National Curriculum, which are then replaced by further booklets as the rules are rewritten again. But what is most galling of all is that the revisions could have been predicted; had anyone cared to listen, precisely these criticisms were being made in 1987 and 1988, when this was all supposedly in the planning stage.

But because the criticisms came from professionals, the despised education lobby which was due for demolition, no-one in power was disposed to listen. The juggernaut of the Thatcher government rolled on, remorseless and determined. Painfully, expensively, we learn from their mistakes, because nobody could teach these people anything.

One result of this fitful history has been to give us a curriculum without balance. Teachers in junior schools, battered with contradictory and escalating demands, have had precious little help in how to construct a coherent school day for their pupils. In secondary schools there are damaging differences between the impact of NC on various subject departments. There was an early official enthusiasm, for Maths, Science and Technology, partly because it was assumed that these subjects would be economically productive. So working groups were set up, and produced elaborate demands and early deadlines.

By comparison, the arts were devalued. Drama was absorbed within English, Dance assimilated into PE, and on the same vague economic criteria the discussion of the arts was postponed as presumably less urgent. There was no attempt to calculate their value as an educational experience. We need to think not just about "what the country needs" (i.e. job vacancies), but also "what's in a child's week at school ?" and "what is it that will help them to grow ?" The consequence of the NC's implementation was to reduce the time, money and teachers devoted to the arts, but nowhere was this advanced as a rational argument. It just turned out that way.

A current booklet from the DES promises parents that all pupils will study English, maths,science, technology, a modern foreign language and PE up to 16. In addition

" they will be able to choose courses leading to qualifications awarded by vocational bodies like BTEC, City and Guilds and RSA. These courses will cover skills that will help them prepare for a particular kind of job or further training;

they will be able to choose between history and geography, or take shorter courses in both;*

they will be able to choose whether to carry on with music and art, or give up one or both;*

they will be able to take up new subjects - for example economics, or another language. "
(Your Child and the NC, DES, 1991, p. 9)

This is staggering. The two asterisks indicate that "The Government is consulting on these proposals before seeking Parliamentary approval", presumably because they already contravene the existing regulations of the Education Reform Act. The consultation, though, needs to be a lot more basic than that.

They might, for instance, talk to a head teacher. If you have 60 pupils in a year, you can offer them three - or perhaps four - options at any one time. So that you might have 20 pupils doing history, 15 doing geography, and 25 doing a mixture of the two. If, on the other hand, you have a larger school, with 300 pupils in the year, you can (on the same ratio) offer 15-20 different courses. This is not a question of educational dogma, but of economics; how many teachers have you got, and how small can you afford your classes to be ? (What happens if only 10 pupils pick Geography ? Do you run it,or not ?)

There is simply no chance of many schools being able to offer the full range of possibilities outlined in this pamphlet, yet it is being widely distributed before any teacher has the chance to respond.

And what's so good about choice ? One of the results of choice has been that our brightest pupils, entering A level courses, often choose not to do science. What is a perfectly reasonable personal choice leaves us on a national scale with a less scientifically aware population than we apparently need - and certainly this was part of industry's initial enthusiasm for the NC project.

The aim was never very clear - Were there particular scientific jobs unfilled ? Did we need to divert able pupils from arts subjects into sciences ? Or were we after a whole population that was more scientifically aware ? Nobody was quite sure, and it didn't seem to matter. So now the undermining of combined science, the passionate emphasis on choice and the obsessive concern to retain specialist A levels in their present form will together ensure that on the scientific front nothing much will change.

In Technology, there has been much confusion and some educational enthusiasm, but here again the serious thinking was not done. If we were genuinely scientific, we would construct a hypothesis, carry out an experiment and study the results; if we were truly technological, we would evaluate the proposed model before assuming that it met the demands of the nation.

It doesn't. Technology for all is an exciting idea, but with existing staffing and resources it can only be taught to all pupils if they focus on the process - and follow a technological route through a variety of media with a team of varied specialists. That's an interesting, ambitious journey, but it creates little enthusiasm among some professional technologists, who suspect what they see as an abstract generalisation of the design process, and a consequent decline in the level of technical skill.

So, on one of the key criteria - relevance to work, and national competitiveness - there is no reason to suspect that our future system will be very different from what it has always been. I suspect many employers will end up saying that there was a lot of fuss about nothing.

# CHAPTER FOUR: Education for All ?

## THE SELECTIVE OBSESSION

It goes back to Plato.

"You are, all of you in this land, brothers. But when God fashioned you, he added gold in the composition of those of you who are qualified to be Rulers..; he put silver in the Auxiliaries, and iron and bronze in the farmers and the rest." (The Republic, trans. H.D.P.Lee, Penguin, 1955, p.160)

Gold, silver, bronze. Upper class, middle class, working class. Grammar, Technical, Secondary. A stream, B stream, C stream. These levels and divisions have been a distinctive feature of English society and education (and it is peculiarly English, since the Scots arrange things differently, and in many ways better). We have focussed on the business of selection - Matriculation, 11 plus, scholarships, entrance examinations - sometimes at the expense of the actual learning. Because of our class structure, we have been more concerned to identify and accentuate differences, than to define a common heritage to which all can lay claim.

Sometimes this process has been justified intellectually. The Norwood report of 1943 argued that "The evolution of education has thrown up certain groups, each of which can and must be treated in a way appropriate to itself."

There is the intellectual, the technically able, and the pupil "who deals more easily with concrete things than with ideas." This was the justification for an honest concerned attempt to provide suitably different provision, at three different types of school - Grammar, Technical and Secondary Modern. The hope was that there would be "parity of esteem", that these types would be seen as equal but different, but once more some were more equal than others.

The 11 plus did not distinguish types of ability, but successes and failures. Prestige, entrance to university, access to responsible jobs and qualified staff went overwhelmingly in one direction, so parental approval followed. The result was that a narrow model of academic excellence became identified as 'the best'; engineers and retailers were seen as inferior to professors or diplomats, and any attempt to change any part of the academic route - A levels, degree courses, Oxbridge - was fiercely resisted. Parity of esteem was always an illusion, one more casualty of the English passion to select.

There is another way of doing things. We could say - "Every child needs an education. Everyone needs the best education possible. Education is not a privilege, for a particular class of people, for successful candidates or for the winners of a lottery. It is a right. Education is for all."

At times, we have said that, or tried to say it. The Education Acts of 1870 and 1944, the growth of comprehensive schools, the development of community education and mixed-ability teaching - all these were moves (sometimes faltering, sometimes flawed ) in the direction of a universal service. And most other countries with our degree of development, but without our hierarchical obsessions, have adopted such a view, seeing the practical advantages as well as the moral value of providing education for all.

In England, though, we have found it difficult. This may be rooted in the history of our schools, which have developed over centuries by catering for an increasing range of particular groups - for monks and priests, an officer class for the empire, the children of the rich, members of religious denominations, and so on.

In such a tradition, independence comes to be highly valued - sometimes at the cost of justice. Public schools are defended as "the right of parents to spend their money how they like." But how absolute is this ? Which privileges should money convey - better health ? more influence at elections ? a higher chance of success in the law courts ? access to a better class of road ? In education, the result is that some children get a much more expensive education than others, and this may or may not be right, but the insistent defence of that discrepancy is peculiarly English. This shows in the attempts to compare the educational performance between school pupils of different nationalities; we are often fed reports of these, as further evidence of our decline, but the key finding is that there is a wider difference between the performances of English pupils than between those of other nationalities.

We have then, two rival images of education - is this a market in which customers shop around for quality, or a system which provides for all ? If it's a market, then there should be a variety of provision, lots of different sorts of schools on offer, and parents should shop around to find the best. If it's a system, then we have to provide good quality learning for all children, and manage resources as effectively as we can. It may not be an absolute choice, and there may be times when the market is also a system, but time and again the crunch of educational decision-making arrives, and politicians are forced to choose - market or system ?

This looks on the surface like a simple political split - Conservative market against Labour system - but it hasn't worked out that way. The division may apply between extreme theoreticians but in practice, in government, there has been little to choose between them.

Conservative politicians protested about the rate of comprehensivisation under Labour, but they then continued the process (because the 11 plus was unpopular, and many voters were in favour of its abolition). Labour leaders have been strong on the rhetoric of justice and equality, but have shown little inclination to challenge the status quo of 'independent' education, the benefits of the affluent. And now, when the conviction politics of Mrs. Thatcher has encouraged a more partisan approach to the government of education, by no means all Conservatives are in favour:
"A South Shropshire school governor and former Tory activist has resigned his post, saying 'I have simply had enough of these crackpot policies..Education has been hit by change after change, and has become the political battleground between the two old parties. And in the middle of the whole mess - let us not forget it - are the children, and the parents who want something for those children.' "
(Liberal Democrat election leaflet, Ludlow constituency 1992)

The key figures in the recent history of our education service are distinguished more by personality, commitment and style, than by party. Edward Boyle, a Conservative, did wonders for the morale of teachers and 'the system', mainly by effort and good manners - visiting schools, talking to people in them, and valuing the work that they did. Antony Crosland provided the necessary commitment and courage to push through comprehensivisation, because of his personal qualities rather than any party commitment ( the Crossman diaries dispose of any illusion that the Wilson Government as a whole had any serious strategy for education). Both ministers strengthened the notion of a system, a service for all.

With these exceptions, little was done to disturb the fundamental compromise until 1979. Whichever party was in power would make occasional friendly noises, but would take little interest in education and would allocate responsibility for it to someone who was neither able nor expected to make much difference. (Mrs. Thatcher's "snatching" of free school milk gained her notoriety, but is hardly an exception. Had she carried out her intentions for nursery education, the story would be very different). There was a general consensus that education would tick over, give or take the occasional crisis, and that even if governments wanted to change it, the machinery wasn't there.

Such a situation could not survive Mrs. Thatcher's rise to power. Her previous experience of the DES made her suspicious enough of civil servants in action, and as the confidence of her government grew so did the Ministerial attempts to change how things were done.

This was ironic, as both Mrs. Thatcher and Keith Joseph were happier with the 'market' model than the 'system'; in their ideal world, good schools would be encouraged to develop quality learning as best suited them, and the weakest would go to the wall, but they happened to have inherited a system, so they might as well reform it.

Most of Joseph's initiatives were directed at the few, at selecting quality (whether of teachers or taught). Following American experiments, he wanted to reward particularly skillful teachers, and he was most anxious that the new GCSE arrangements should allow for particular recognition for the most able pupils. On the other hand, he had a genuine concern for pupils whose attainments were lower than their potential, and he was rightly anxious to reduce the extent to which school was a boring experience.

Unfortunately, he not only had to work under the shadow of a bitter pay dispute, but also in a climate which had been soured by a steady stream of disparagement, whereby Government ministers consistently publicised their misgivings about the performance of the education system.

Views about the effectiveness of criticism vary - although there is some interesting evidence from schools about the relative merits of praise and blame in motivating pupils. What is certain is that large numbers of teachers under Sir Keith Joseph felt devalued, with their efforts despised, resources reduced and the parents of the children they taught being encouraged to find fault with their work.

Enter Kenneth Baker, a very different sort of performer. He also was a an educated man, with intellectual interests, but he lacked Joseph's disabling self-doubt, and as a past supporter of Edward Heath he was determined to demonstrate the zeal of a convert to Thatcherism. The teaching dispute had been

42

damaging, and indicated a profession working in murkily defined conditions where "withdrawal of goodwill" could apparently bring things to a standstill.

Baker's task was to remedy this situation, and to convince parents that they were being offered widespread improvements in education. The result was the Education Reform Act.

A UNIVERSAL PACKAGE ?

What is surprising is the universal nature of the package. The outline of the curriculum being offered echoed previous work from HMI and the DES, and resembled what some schools were already offering - a large core of compulsory subjects (English, Maths, Double Science, Technology, Languages for All) and greatly reduced scope for options. This may have been conviction, or pragmatism - school rolls were falling, and it is harder for small schools with fewer staff to run a full range of optional subjects - but whatever the motives the original Baker package was a radical guarantee to all pupils that they would get the same, quality education.

This came as a surprise to many teachers, a welcome one to those who believed in a comprehensive system, and a serious threat to those who preferred the open market principle. But it gradually became clear that both these reactions were premature, since the real thinking had not been done, and the logical consequences of the reform therefore came as an unpleasant surprise to its author.

Take Science, for example. Quite independently of government discussions, a movement had been growing to replace the old separate Science Options (Chemistry, Physics and Biology) with a course for all pupils which would contain elements of these three, co-ordinated or combined. The combined Science lobby argued that all pupils should undergo this study, which would amount to 20% of timetable time (four double lessons a week), and would in most cases lead to the award of two GCSE grades (hence Double Science).

There was a concession that a few pupils might only manage a single certificate, perhaps in 12.5% of timetable time, but there was a strong concern that girls should not be able to opt out of a commitment to Science, or choose Biology as a means of evading the discipline of Physics and Chemistry.

Kenneth Baker seemed to have accepted this argument, by incorporating the double science demand as part of the compulsory core, a legal requirement of the National Curriculum. Then, somewhere along the line, he changed his mind.

Not all science teachers were happy with the Combined Science package. Some feared a loss of traditional rigour, and science teachers in independent schools argued strongly, and successfully, for the retention of the old disciplines. "We are in the position", a union leader commented, "of the national curriculum dog being wagged by the private sector tail."

There were also representatives of other subjects - classics and home economics, for instance, excluded from the NC outline -who were worried that there would be no space left for them. So the government commitment to Combined Science suddenly evaporated, and by September 1990 a NCC planning paper could seriously suggest that "Schools offering model B (12.5 %) Science would have additional flexibility." (Planning for Keystage 4; a supplementary paper, 1990, p.3) In other words, cut down your science commitment and there's room to do other things.

The argument is not about whether this was a correct decision; the point is, the change of mind is from a confident assertion of universal entitlement, to a more laissez-faire approach: these are the possibilities, you sort out what you want to do.

A similar dilution undermined the commitment to Languages. As with Combined Science, there was a strong movement towards Languages for All, before the National Curriculum was thought of. All pupils, it was said, should continue to study languages throughout their secondary school careers; and we could not afford for pupils who were unsuccessful or unhappy in Language work simply to opt out of it.

Given our increasing commitment to Europe, this was a reasonable case (but also a courageous one, bearing in mind the academic nature of much language teaching, and the challenges involved in teaching languages to all sixteen year olds throughout the country). And again, it seemed that Mr. Baker had been won over, so that the National Curriculum was endorsing radical developments already taking place. But again, he hadn't read the small print.

First, if all pupils do languages, most schools will need more language teachers, since the option system currently allows many to choose other subjects instead. Second, if NC fills up all the time (ten subjects, for 10% of the time each), how does anyone ever learn two languages ? Where are the linguists of the future to come from, let alone the new language teachers for the year 2000 ?

While these proposals were being discussed, Mr. Baker made a quick trip to Russia, stopping just long enough to lament that so few schools study Russian. But if all pupils are to do a language,and only one language, then the chances of those pupils studying Russian are very small indeed.

As it was, Mr. Baker's advisers looked at the commitment, worried about the supply of language teachers, gulped and postponed the deadlines. Yes, languages for all is a nice idea, but we may not be able to do it with everyone, or at any rate just not yet.

This process of retreat from entitlement accelerated under Kenneth Clarke. On January 4th., 1991, he told the North of England Conference:
"I believe we should not impose on them a rigid curriculum that leaves little scope for choice."
(That was precisely what Kenneth Baker had set out to do: "Three core subjects and seven other foundation subjects which must be included in the curricula of all pupils...")
Kenneth Clarke outlined the "sensible choices" he thinks pupils might want to make:
"Some pupils might want to study three separate sciences, or a second or third modern language or the classics. Others might want to contemplate pre-vocational courses in technical, economic or business-oriented subjects aimed at qualifications such as BTEC. It is simply not possible to have both the 10 course set menu and the kind of provision for RE, which I know many of you want, for every pupil, plus the à la carte selections for some. A decision has to be made that leans one way or the other. I have decided, and I have inclined towards more flexibility and choice for these older pupils, their parents and teachers. It is quite clear that John MacGregor was inclining in the same direction."

It is also quite clear that the National Curriculum was originally defined in precisely the opposite direction. And it has subsequently been made clear (by Duncan Graham, then Chair and Chief Executive of the NCC) that the government's own appointed body, the NCC, was not consulted abut the change. Their previous advice was ignored, and the Chairman was only informed the night before Clarke's speech of the bombshell he was about to drop.

In PE, the working group recommended that at the end of key stage 2 "children should be able to show that they can swim at least 25 metres, and know about and demonstrate water safety. " This was not just a whim; a serious group of people looked at eleven institutions in this country, made comparisons with the PE taught in France, Germany and Sweden, and thought it reasonable to propose that we set a national target of every child being able to swim before the age of 11. The savings on accidents, drownings and grief would be considerable, let alone the gains in personal confidence.

This was Mr. Clarke's reply:
"It is not part of the Group's remit to make recommendations for the resources to be provided for PE. I expect your recommendations to be realistically related to the general level of school funding which can reasonably be expected to be available."

Some will get it, some won't, depending on proximity to swimming pools, availability and cost of transport, parental backing - and luck. This is one area where a national commitment, a piece of creative compulsion, could have enhanced the quality of life, but Clarke was prepared to miss the chance.

Where this choice arises, it is now likely that the market will prevail, and the secretary of state will retreat from any commitment to universal provision - especially if cost is involved. There are difficult questions here, of freedom and responsibility. By what right do we decide that a bright girl who does not like science should do science ? Can a talented boy do Music and Art at GCSE, and if not why not ? How can we have a truly national curriculum where the subjects offered vary with money, staffing and the size of school ?

Another tangled area concerns statemented pupils. Since the Education Act of 1981 there have been moves to identify the needs of pupils with learning difficulties, and to try to direct resources specifically towards them. There have also been moves towards integrating such pupils as fully as possible within mainstream classes, so that they have the maximum chance of being involved in 'normal' work.

The NC definition followed in this tradition of entitlement, arguing that such pupils were entitled to the full range of NC subjects (rather than a limited diet of remedial exercises). What it failed to do was to face the problem of resourcing. If a pupil is entitled to individual attention in a small group, but is also entitled to Science teaching by a Science specialist, how does a school ensure that both needs are met without some increase in its staffing ?

In practice, as the National Curriculum has developed, so it has moved further and further away from children least likely to achieve success. The rhetoric says that this is education for all, but it is actually education for the verbally fluent, for the confident thinker who can flit happily between subjects. In this intricate verbal labyrinth, most of our least able pupils will simply be lost without trace.


## THE DOMINANT PATTERN

I do not ask pupils to vote on whether 'ouvert' is French for 'open'. I do not send them on the cross-Channel ferry to mime opening gestures and come back with an answer. I tell them. I may even write it on the blackboard, and get them to copy it down.

But that is not all I do. I want these pupils to be able to speak French for themselves. I want them to meet French people and talk with them freely, and gain the benefits of seeing how other people live. Some of these things they will have to practice, learn and discover, initiating conversations as well as responding to my lead. I can't just tell them.

So, what I do and how I teach will vary, but one of the factors which will influence my calculations is how people work. People work better when they see some purpose in what they are doing, when they are allowed to understand the context and have some say in how the job is done. Managers in industry know this, even if politicians don't, and it certainly applies in school.

Some work is difficult, and some work is repetitive. There is no special virtue in these things, and part of the teaching art is to render work as interesting and varied as possible, while still insisting that some challenges have to be faced, some difficulties overcome.

As a teacher, I am responsible for what goes on in my lessons. For any learning to take place I will need order, and sometimes (reading, intensive writing) I will require total silence. Sometimes I want pupils to talk to each other, or to the whole class, and I may also want them to go to the library, interview a shopkeeper or show a visitor round school. My demands will vary, and so will the kind of control I exercise.

Whether a particular approach is too demanding, or insufficiently challenging, or exciting but irrelevant - these are not simple judgements. They have to be made each day, by teachers, but they depend on a number of factors: the pupils, the material, the teacher themselves, the work that has gone before and the work that lies ahead. What is certain is that it will not help to have confident generalisations shouted from a distance, by politicians who are confident that this work can be simplified:

"Some people hold the rather curious view that teaching knowledge one person to another is a rather authoritarian activity. The education world is full of people who get frightfully upset by that kind of language."

The tone suggests that this is all very simple really, but that teachers are making it difficult. Kenneth Clarke was happy with the traditional patterns of dominance, as a simple model. For him, quality is secured by keeping control of what is taught, and is threatened by mass participation. 'We' must make sure that 'they' get what is required:

"Prince Charles is correct when he asserts that we do not know how much Shakespeare is currently taught. We don't, and we won't till 1992 when that part of the English curriculum comes into play. At 14 we will be sure every child will be studying at least one or two Shakespeare plays..."

Like a measles jab, like penalties for spelling, Shakespeare is inflicted, to keep them in their place - or rather, in their separate places, for Kenneth Clarke also proclaimed that he was " all in favour of streaming." That this only makes a significant difference in very large schools did not seem to matter; it is the very process of selection which reassures.

Any class will contain variations in ability - different kinds of intelligence, levels of ability, fluctuating motivation, a fluid spectrum of personality and social background. Teachers acknowledge this diversity, even thrive on it, provided they are free to respond. Approaches have to be varied to secure the best result, but the effect of NC has been to limit that variety.

"One of the points was to get young people interested and excited. Ruling out 20 years of the immediate past undermines the whole edifice." (Martin Roberts, chairman of the Historical Association's Education Committee ).

This 'date-capping' also contradicts the earliest stages of NC History, in which pupils tackling key stage 1 look at their own place in history.

A similar pattern occurred in Geography - "He has taken the subject

backwards by removing the aspects which have made it interesting and popular."
(D. Burtenshaw, secretary of the Geographical Association).

Ten university lecturers wrote:

"It is important that we should be clear about what has happened: a politician, ignoring professional advice, has used wide-ranging powers to outline what pupils should learn. In the place of argued academic and professional opinion, the prejudices of a politician have intruded directly into the school curriculum." (Letter to The Guardian, 23.1.91)

That sounds like a serious charge. But there was no response, or visible public outcry. We seem to have got used to doing things this way.

Kenneth Clarke was not unaware of these criticisms. He was actually proud of them, in stamping him as the preserver of traditional standards, high quality, unpopular work:
"Educationists have criticised my old-fashioned insistence on content in the history and geography syllabuses."

"Educationists" sound stuffy, distant experts with an irrelevant axe to grind. But Clarke's changes were also attacked by teachers, whose job it was to present this material in the classroom. If you're a teacher, you don't strike an ideological attitude and turn it into a statue. You work on something, and then try to fill in the bits that have been left out. You use real books, and phonics; provide stimulus, and check the spellings; you teach the whole class, and you differentiate. While Kenneth Clarke was engaged in ideological warfare, we are involved in a much subtler, more complex operation - but for how long will we retain the freedom to respond with professional judgement ?

UNIFORM PROGRESS ?

It is curious that this traditional, elitist concern for dominance should foster a myth of uniformity, an abstract vision of conveyor-belt learning:
"By eleven they will be able to read different kinds of texts and make comparisons between them. They will begin to match their style of writing to different audiences. They will be getting better at organising their work, punctuation, spelling and putting their ideas across clearly...By 14 pupils will be able to discuss and summarise what they have read, including plays and poems from earlier centuries. They will be able to write independently and at length for

different purposes - reviews, letters, essays, reports, playscripts, stories."
("Your Child and the NC", DES Dec '91, pp. 6 and 8)

Though if they're all doing this at the same rate, you begin to wonder why anyone talks about streaming. These are, don't forget, the children you see on the streets, and on television - delivering papers, playing football, hanging around and going on sponsored walks. They are the computer freaks and the vandals, the young musicians and the joyriders, the ecological campaigners and the victims of child abuse - all working their way through the levels together.

We all want value for money, and teacher expectations for all pupils should be high. But the way of securing that is not to imply a standard route down which all pupils will proceed at an identical speed. Things are not as simple as that, and it is dishonest to pretend that they are.

The promise of universal provision will not be kept, but the wonder is that it was ever made at all. So much of our pattern is piecemeal, that it is astonishing that any government, let alone a Conservative government, should have come so close to a commitment in the first place. They as a party, and we as a country, are uneasy with blanket provision (with the single, endangered exception of the National Health Service).

Consider, for example, nursery education, once singled out by Mrs. Thatcher as a crucial universal requirement. In Italy and parts of the USA, authorities decide that all children are entitled to good nursery education, and they literally count the gains: more chance of employment, better pay, greater educational success; less crime, less need for special education or social benefit. For this is not an expensive moral gesture; it is ultimately a financial saving, self-interest as well as common sense. We, meanwhile, persist in our patchwork quilt of minders and schools, playgroups and informal arrangements, some public, some private, financed to varying degrees from different sources and with wildly sporadic effect. For all the talk of management, we lack the willpower for the right decisive action, the courage to spend money now in order to save it later.

So perhaps it was always a dream that all our children would follow the same route. That they would study the same subjects through the same four key stages, that they would simultaneously pursue the same attainment targets across the land, registering achievement in a way that would instantly be recognisable to parents of all types of background. Did they ever mean it, truly ?

It is hard to be sure. It was always a little bit strange that the National Curriculum was voluntary for independent schools. If it's that good, surely everyone should have it ? If teachers in private schools can do better, why can't state teachers have a try at doing better ? A government which could erase the negotiating rights of teachers, and sack trade unionists at GCHQ, surely need not be coy about imposing the National Curriculum on independent schools. After all, if the law's a problem, you just change the law. It's been done before.

Perhaps they weren't quite sure that they'd got it right. But if they weren't sure, they could surely have stopped for breath, paused  - for reflection, or even consultation - before proceeding to legislate. And that pause for thought might then have enabled them seriously to consider, and answer, a crucial question. Is this whole expensive, erratic venture a public relations exercise, a sop for those who can't afford private schooling, or do we want an educated society ? Are we, or are we not, providing education for all ?

# CHAPTER FIVE; The Tower of Babel

## THE PLAYERS

Where did the National Curriculum come from ?

That may seem like a strange question, and I have offered one answer already - it was a politician's response to a political problem. But although Kenneth Baker's role was crucial, he did not sit down and personally compose the requirements of the National Curriculum. So who did, and how did they do it?

It is much easier to pose that question than to answer it. What can be done, however, is to briefly outline the main characters in this complex drama, who are usually identified by their acronyms.

The Department of Education and Science (DES), now renamed DFE (Department for Education), contains civil servants whose role it is to carry out policy defined by the Secretary of State. As is usual these days, that involves a mixture of career civil servants, and advisers close to the current cabinet or minister, who finally have a precious opportunity to put theories into practice.

The Secretary of State could also call on Her Majesty's Inspectors (HMI), traditionally an independent group ( owing loyalty to the Crown, rather than to a specific government). HMI were former teachers, with their own expertise in subject areas, who were also experienced observers of education. They ran inspections of schools, but also made regular visits to enable them to report on a whole range of educational issues - discipline, attendance and truancy, personal and social education, the state of school buildings, and so on.

Their traditional image has been of suited, respectable observers, sometimes conservative in their assumptions but careful, objective and intelligent. Their reports could be dull but were never silly, and their best work has been helpful, even inspiring - "Aspects of Secondary Education" is a fascinating overall view of work in secondary schools.

Under Mrs. Thatcher's government, however, they  had an increasingly bumpy ride. The independence which enabled them to comment on the effects of financial cuts was not well received in Cabinet, and increasingly tough pressure was exerted to prevent them from speaking freely. HMI certainly contributed to the definition of the National Curriculum, but they were not in charge of the process, and many of them have reservations about it which have not been aired. Current government plans, though, are for the inspectorate to be effectively disbanded.

Teachers have never had an equivalent of the BMA, a central body which could claim to speak for the profession. The nearest approach was probably the Schools Council, which was not perfect but did produce some good materials and useful publications, and had the advantage of being in some sense representative.

The Schools Council was an early casualty of the Thatcher Government, whose appetite for democratic representation was severely restricted. In its place they eventually appointed two bodies, to deal respectively with the content of the curriculum, and its assessment. ( This dangerous split, encouraging work on assessment which was not related to teaching, was attacked by professionals when the two groups were set up, in 1987. In 1992, as part of John Patten's White Paper, the two groups became one. No explanation, no apology, just five years of expensive argument).

The National Curriculum Council (NCC) was set up to oversee the definition and running of the National Curriculum, and it was not simply composed of educationists. This is reasonable, given the laudable aim of making the curriculum accessible and acceptable to employers and parents, as well as to teachers. It meant, though, that there was very little direct experience of teaching in the Council itself.

This was to be balanced by the appointment of officers, recruited from teachers and educational administrators, and the creation of subject working groups - which included practising teachers, relevant outsiders and senior figures appointed by the government. John Fashanu, a professional footballer, was in the PE group, and Mike Batt, a musician, worked on the submission for Music.

There is also a more permanent staff of educational professionals. Lay people sometimes assume that these must be the best of their field, but that is not always the case. There are some very talented people within the NC staff, but they operate under severe restrictions. Some undoubtedly work to ensure the best possible deal for school pupils, but others are drawn by the short-term rewards, the self-importance and the sense of power. There is in the nature of NCC work an appeal to plausible, rootless performers which makes it unlikely that they will retain close links with schools. Such contact is further discouraged by their Stalinist conditions of service, which preclude open discussion and honest exchange.

Assessment was the responsibility of the Schools Examination and Assessment Council (SEAC), whose brief was to regulate the complex world of examinations, and ultimately to co-ordinate existing qualifications (the GCSE in particular) with the new assessment requirements of the National Curriculum. Here, too, there are competent professionals, and there would be real gains in having somewhere an independent body of full-time, qualified experts in assessment. We used to have the Assessment of Performance Unit, then we had SEAC, but that has been castrated by political intervention, and is now to be merged with the NCC.

Behind the scenes, but not that far behind, was the Centre for Policy Studies (CPS), a rightwing pressure group with no statutory power but considerable influence on this particular government.

So far, then, we have the DES, HMI, NCC, SEAC and the CPS. Each of these had a part to play, but there was no complete copy of the script. Rehearsal time was short, a good deal of improvisation took place, and for spectators it was very difficult to work out what was happening.

The earliest versions of the National Curriculum, for instance, took almost no account of Personal and Social Education. Teachers responsible for PSE were gloomy at the sudden demise of what had seemed to be a fruitful development; and yet now there is the commitment to promote " the spiritual, moral, cultural, mental and physical development of pupils." Such cross-curricular themes as Health Education and Careers are to be carefully charted across the curriculum of every school. The change is welcome, but it happened fast, and with no explanation.

The best recent example of the hydra-headed monster in action is the revision of the NC regulations concerning Music. The Music working party produced a report which was widely welcomed, with 83% of the 1,707 responses from musical and teaching organisations expressing approval. Kenneth Clarke, however, felt that insufficient stress had been laid on the history and traditions of music.

The recommendations went before the National Curriculum Council, who then appeared to require certain changes. The number of attainment targets was reduced, a list of Western composers was added, and the multi-cultural scope of the music to be played was severely limited. This new report was issued to the press before a copy had been received by Sir John Manduell, Chairman of the working party.

A large number of prominent musicians appealed directly to the Prime Minister, opposing the changes and asking him to intervene. Simon Rattle said the changes " would be the greatest disaster for music in Britain in my lifetime" and spoke against them at his concerts. Sir John Manduell, in a moment of honest defiance rare in the furtive history of the NC, commented:
"The Council is flying in the face of professional opinion to a breathtaking degree. It is quite clear from what we know that the council declined to make the decision that they were being encouraged to make and left it to the chairman."

This is a blatantly political operation. It is confusing, but the simple fact to grasp is that this is an argument about music, all the musicians are on the same side, and at the moment they seem likely to lose. That could change, though, because the final decision lies somewhere between the working party...the National Curriculum Council...the Secretary of State...and the Prime Minister. That's how this curriculum is defined.

From the start, such confusion has been a regular feature. Paperwork arrived by the lorry load, but deadlines were not kept to, and the air was thick with rumour. Staff came back from conferences with hints, leaks and suggestions, while head teachers had to rely on personal contacts and the "Times Educational Supplement". Utterances from HMI would appear to contradict proposals from the NCC, and then SEAC would come up with something else again.
Part of the game's confusion was explained by the number of players, and the failure to define their roles. Part of it stemmed from the atmosphere of secretive haste which was a distinctive feature of the Thatcher government - us against them, we have to do all we can while we have the power, in case they get back in and ruin it. But part of it derived from the way in which the thinking was done.

For the construction of the National Curriculum was profoundly uneducational. Education involves a tension, between authority and exploration. You have to learn what has been learnt and discovered by others, take in the thoughts and actions of previous learners - otherwise each of us re-invents the wheel and wastes a lot of time. On the other hand, there has to be the room for each learner to question and explore, to create hypotheses which have not yet been tested, to look at old assumptions in a new light. In short, to innovate.

What was strange about the National Curriculum is that it did neither of these things. It did not go back to theories of education, to Plato or Dewey or Rousseau. It did not appeal to current thinkers, Bruner or Bantock, Holt or Hargreaves. Nor did it make use of the best of current practice. One intelligent approach, you might think, would be to look at some good schools, analyse what they did, and then try to replicate that work across the country. Not a bit of it.

On the other hand, doing your own thing also involves knowing your own mind. If you don't want to be distracted by the past, but are setting up something new and original, then you should at least justify what you do. The current National Curriculum regards Drama as a part of English. It requires all pupils to study science to the age of 16, but not history. It encourages the combining of science, but not the combining of humanities. What are the reasons for these decisions ?

They are not spelt out, and you often get different accounts from different voices, because the responsibility is variously divided, and full, rational argument is positively discouraged. We have the ironic spectacle of a government imposing a pattern of education in an unthinking and irrational way. It should be no surprise that the result is less than satisfactory.

As time passes, so the truth emerges. Gradually people gather the courage to defy the ferocious and irrational demand for secrecy. Ken Dobson, chief examiner for Nuffield advanced Physics, was a member of the original science working party:
"The penultimate version of physics in the national curriculum was so bad and full of howlers that it had to be completely rewritten. Then the rewriting was done in less than three days by just one person! I know because it was me."
(Article in "The Guardian", 31.3.92)

And matters have apparently not improved:
"The Secretary of State and the subserviently vapid science committee of SEAC don't know what they are doing. They do not understand the system they have created or approved. Committee members seem unwilling to give advice based on their professional judgements - they simply agree to official dictate. It is an amazing example of centralised bureaucracy."

This is not a particular error. It is a way of working which is intrinsically unsound, and which is unlikely to improve simply with practice, by letting the time go by.

With each month that passes, more of the cracks appear. As I revised this chapter in August 1992, Professor Paul Black's address to the British Association was reported. Professor Black chaired the TGAT group, which was responsible for the early outlines of NC assessment. This is his appraisal of the present situation:

"The current ideas are based on prejudice rather than evidence, and are set fair to do harm to children's education..We really are in very profound trouble. If the teaching profession's practices and judgements are no longer to be trusted, then the fault cannot be corrected simply by giving them new orders. They are not robots."

From a senior government adviser, recognised by them as an expert, that looks like a serious charge. "The Guardian" clearly thought so, since it headed their front page (26.8.92) , but nobody else seemed bothered. The interesting response is that of Baroness Blatch, Education Minister of State.

"It is sad that Professor Black who had contributed so much to the development of the national curriculum in the past is now so badly out of touch. Pupils and their parents are entitled to higher standards now, not at some indeterminate time in the future, and they would certainly not thank us for delaying the reforms unnecessarily just to allow the academics more time for debate."

Kenneth Clarke has moved on, but his spirit lives. Never mind the quality, feel the haste. Quite apart from the intriguing possibility that Baroness Blatch is "in touch" with something educational denied to Professor Black, she simply does not grasp the point. "Academics" in her view are just wasting time, postponing action; it simply does not occur to her that the academics are identifying what is wrong with government action, are showing why it does not, will not and cannot succeed.

Mill, for one, would have got the point:
"The whole strength and value, then, of human judgement, depending on the one property, that it can be set right when it is wrong..."

# LANGUAGE

Much effort and expense have gone into explaining the National Curriculum. "From Policy to Practice" argued that "the flow of information... can help to raise standards of achievement and understanding of educational goals."(7.1) Since then there has been no pause in the deluge of paperwork. The National Curriculum Council spends four million pounds a year on advice and materials, with a further £100,000 on newsletters. It views this publishing role with impressive solemnity:

"Council has a major contribution to make to the production and dissemination of these materials. Our aim will be to supply guidance and in-service publications which are designed to offer down to earth, practical support which helps teachers meet the difficulties they are experiencing."
(NCC Corporate Plan, 1991, p.7)

So we're down here, struggling, and they're up there - with a vast budget - handing down the answers. Except that there's no reason why their answers should be right. The NCC does not have the best teachers, or the best practice, or any experience about how to operate the National Curriculum, because it's all been designed from scratch and it's constantly being redefined as we go along. This limits the quality of what they can produce, but it does nothing to stem the flow.

Quantity is not the same as quality. The sheer amount is in fact a deterrent, since only the keenest reader has the stomach for them all. The unstable nature of the art is also a discouragement; why read this now, when it will be out of date in six months ?

But there is also the language. National Curriculum proclaimed itself as a new start, and like a shrewd advertising campaign, coined its own catchphrases. We no longer had third years and syllabuses; we had year 9 and programmes of study, with attainment targets and profile components to bear in mind. The new headings were polysyllabic, like most educational jargon, and they therefore attracted scepticism from many teachers, and sheer incomprehension from outsiders.

This matters more because this package was meant to appeal to outsiders. Bitter jokes in the staffroom about "another file of NC bumf" will not worry the NCC, but they should be disturbed at the failure to dress their baby in attractive clothes. If you want the public to like you, they should see you at their best.

So, what's wrong with the language ?

First of all, there's a lack of honesty. When the Science Working Group introduce their revised report with this comment, it sounds like common sense:
"Under the existing order there are 409 statements of attainment in Science: a number we consider too large for manageable assessment."

They're right. But what they don't say is that there are still 178 statements of attainment left, and that may not be manageable either. They also omit to mention that many science teachers had objected from the outset that the original scheme was unworkable. This was a political concession, not a new insight, but it's produced as if it's the product of wise reflection.

Precisely because this is a political operation, its political character has to be concealed. There is a consistent effort to maintain a detached, impersonal tone, whatever the reality. In the early days, much was uncertain, but the NC still had to give the illusion of careful, detailed planning. A SEAC leaflet, for instance, offered "A GUIDE TO TEACHER ASSESSMENT: Your Questions Answered." It sounds frank and helpful, a positive response.

Here are some examples:

Q: Will teachers be allowed extra help in the classroom during SAT-time?
A: The normal pattern of classroom activity will continue in SAT-time. Support can continue to be provided in the same way as it would if SATs were not being conducted.
(In other words, no.)

Q: Will there be time for adequate moderation or will it deteriorate into solving problem cases ?
A: SEAC believes there needs to be adequate time for proper training in moderation procedures.
(That's not the question. We all believe that. The point is,  what's going to happen, and who's going to pay ?)

Q: What happens if pupils 'fail' an assessment ?
A: This is a misunderstanding. The aim of assessment within the National Curriculum is to determine what pupils have positively achieved, as the basis for the next stage of learning.
(It's a nice ideal, but there will surely be situations where many pupils are tackling particular attainment targets, and not all are achieving them. Why not say so ?)

The aim is right - of meeting anxiety, and responding to specific doubts - but if the response is as woolly and imprecise as this then it makes the situation worse. Teachers reading through such documents move from hope through boredom and frustration into anger.

The political context discourages honesty, and makes optimism compulsory - whatever the circumstances. Just as party speakers must make every election result a triumph for their party, so the NC has to issue regular bulletins on its own success.

This has been an advertising campaign about "quality", so the publicity must ensure that this is what we've got. (The absence of "quality" from the actual documents is one of the great NC mysteries, to which I return in chapter eight). So the SEAC recorder assures its readers that

"New criteria are being prepared by SEAC as relevant statutory orders emerge. The criteria will provide the basis for assuring quality in all such syllabuses." (SEAC recorder no.7)

No, it's not very interesting to read, but they are working hard to reassure you. What this quality is they don't say, but it is very much to do with formal deliberations between important people:

"The Secretary of State has now responded and invited SEAC to proceed with the development of arrangements for ensuring high standards of provision for assessment in key stage 4...The Council has accordingly sought the views of relevant bodies on its draft general principles for quality assurance." (SEAC recorder no.7)

Feeling better now ? It's elusive, because the words go in but don't actually seem to say much. This is from "Assuring Quality", the SEAC newsletter of Spring 1991. Later the same year SEAC issued a leaflet with the confident title "Quality Assured".

What this actually does is describe arrangements for assessing subjects and to list who does what. It does raise some interesting questions, like "How is the quality of examinations assured ?" But the answers are not so good:

"The examining bodies must make sure that the examinations they run are of good quality and meet syllabus intentions. SEAC monitors and evaluates a sample of examinations each year, through a process called 'scrutiny.'"

It's common sense, and it's not new. It's what you would expect exam boards to have been doing for decades, and they have. But the NC industry has to pretend that they've thought it all up for the first time. So, where's the bright new glossy product we were promised in the ads ?'

'FLEXIBILITY'

The National Curriculum's publicity budget has been enormous, but the money has not been well spent. Many publications have been rushed out simply to keep previous rash promises, before there was anything new to say. And for professionals, teachers whose job it is to actually make the thing work, the reams of paper have been depressing and unhelpful.

Even the basic vocabulary is in doubt. Take a word like "flexibility", for instance. It sounds clear enough, a nice adaptable virtue. It suggests room to move and think, an intelligent responsiveness to circumstances. In practice, it has been a useful get-out when the thinking is unclear; on x we're firm and decisive, but on y we're prepared to be flexible. These are some examples of "flexibility" in use, in the National Curriculum:

(a) "The ERA does not require teaching to be provided under the foundation subject headings. Indeed, it deliberately allows flexibility for schools to provide their teaching in a variety of ways." (From Policy to Practice, 1989)

Flexibility here means alternative teaching strategies, working across conventional subject boundaries. That's what it says, but the whole impact of NC has been to reinforce subject boundaries, and to provide a pressure towards creating them where they did not exist before (in primary schools, and in some integrated work in the early secondary years).

(b) "Schools should have reasonable flexibility to plan for all the foundation subjects and RE and for a balanced range of options outside the National Curriculum."
(John MacGregor, speech to CEOs, 25.1.90)

Again we're in the land of pious hopes. Schools should have that room for manoeuvre, but they didn't have it, because the basic definition of the National Curriculum deprived them of that space.

(c) "Flexibility comes from combining subjects, using modular courses..."
(The Whole Curriculum, NCC, March 1990)

This is an amazing piece of wishful thinking, and a good example of the hydra-headed monster in action. This is NCC saying that by putting subjects together schools will be able to accommodate the various demands of National Curriculum. Yet SEAC, another head, is simultaneously purging integrated courses, in the Humanities, for instance. It's a bit rash to timetable a course if you're not allowed to examine it.

(d) "Table 2 offers illustrations of potential flexibility which 5% courses can provide."
(NCC circular 10, May 1990)

This was a late attempt to square the timetable circle, by reducing the size of the sectors. If subjects could be squeezed down to 5% each, then perhaps everyone would be able to fit in everything ?

Mathematically yes, but practically no. In the brief consultations which John MacGregor encouraged, there was massive opposition to the idea of 5% courses. Teachers would see pupils once a week, for just over an hour at most, and experience suggests that that is not a useful basis for covering a subject syllabus. It certainly would not lead to the equivalent of a GCSE certificate. So this "potential flexibility" is actually nothing of the kind.

That is the problem. You can show what is wrong with this stuff, look at the gap between the words on paper and the reality they purport to describe, but it does take time. The effort of close reading is time-consuming, but it is also part of the education business; we are committed to thinking and analysing, and that means analysing what is written and said as well as what is done.

Meanwhile, the craze for flexibility roars on. The NCC's "Planning for Keystage 4" devoted a whole section to it, proclaiming frameworks rather than strait-jackets, underlining the freedom which schools had to decide how much time they could spend on subjects, how to organise the teaching and how to approach the various cross-curricular skills, dimensions and themes.

What schools were not free to do was challenge the assumption of ten levels, reduce the number of attainment targets, create new ones of their own or introduce fresh material into a crowded curriculum. Some things are more flexible than others, and different people exercise different degrees of flexibility.

The grey supplement to "Planning for KS 4" mentioned flexibility 7

times in 6 pages, and also published a letter from John MacGregor which had 5 references in 2 pages. Kenneth Clarke totally changed the approach in many ways, but he too saw the advantages of the F word. Option blocks, apparently, would offer"...more flexibility and choice for older pupils.." and the dilution of the core curriculum is defended as "sensible flexibility."
(Speech to North of England conference, 4.1.91)

Art, Music and PE, it appears, will have "..a more flexible National Curriculum regime.." which prompts the unworthy thought that there might be something inflexible about the provision for Maths and Science. And then we have this mystifying utterance:
"I have no doubt that all pupils should be obliged to continue their physical education in one form or another, but there should be a particularly flexible definition of physical education at keystage 4..."

Now, what on earth does that mean ?

That is, regularly, the reaction. The words are there, they've been printed and circulated, but I don't know know what they're saying. Most teachers -let alone laymen - find much of the NC documentation difficult or frustrating. It is not the difficulty of profound thought, since some of the best work (the English programmes of study, for instance) is also a pleasure to read. It is the difficulty of vagueness, jargon and political compromise, and it is yet one more reason why the NC is less likely to succeed.

Perhaps as a result, there has been less public criticism of the National Curriculum than you might expect. Opposition MPs have been happy to attack Secretaries of State and particular measures, but the overall edifice has survived unscathed, with occasional, honourable exceptions. There was Cardinal Hume's attack on the utilitarian basis of the NC:
"Not all study has to be at the service of some utilitarian purpose. Simply to know and rejoice in knowing is sufficient justification for study."

But the general tone has been respectful, and most media coverage has solemnly passed on the details - keystages, dates and content of syllabuses - without actually passing judgement. Perhaps it is all too complicated, or perhaps the idea is so attractive that nobody wants to throw stones, but in terms of public discussion the NC has had an easy ride.

# RESOURCES

From the expenditure on documents and public relations, you would expect this to be a well-resourced development. Improving the quality of education for all pupils from 5-16 could well be an expensive process, and the investment of public money on teaching resources would make sense. But this wasn't part of the plan.

"From Policy to Practice" anticipated this argument, and assured its readers that "The requirements will be far from totally new. Most will be familiar ground to teachers, and will build firmly on good practice which is supported to a great extent by existing materials and books." (4.15)

Or, to put it simply, no cash. Primary teachers were to approach the teaching of science with a fresh enthusiasm and rigour, but this was not to be supported by the widespread provision of laboratories in their schools.

The publishers were not impressed with the government's suggestion that this would involve no new resources. The dream of improvement on the cheap, quality without expense, was no use for selling books. So now every educational course, whether specially devised or dragged out of the grave, is presented as essential for the completion of the National Curriculum. B TEC Foundation, the Easy Enterprise Publishing Kit, it doesn't matter; these are what you need, and the more persuasive will even identify the attainment targets at which they are aimed. NatProf, the complete NC profiling system, is not only a user-friendly computerised record-keeping system, but "frees teachers to teach." Now there's a bonus.

The Alton Towers theme park has always been famous for its "white knuckle rides." Now it provides an added attraction - "teacher's resource material on a range of subjects related to the National Curriculum." And yes, the video is available - "National Curriculum Mathematics course for children aged 12-14 years", presenting "highly acclaimed traditional teaching", from "the Tutor you can rewind."

The resources are there, and fresh ones are published daily, but they are not being paid for by the government. Kenneth Clarke was dismissive about the effect of expenditure on learning:

"If you have 10% of pupils with real difficulty reading you can't make them read better by spending more money on them. You have to organise the service so that the teaching is more successful."

It is true that some good education can also be cheap to provide. It is true that mindless expenditure for its own sake does not inevitably bring educational benefit (although the government which gave us City Technology Colleges is not ideally placed to teach us this wise economy). But it is also true that some gains have to be paid for.

To take Mr. Clarke's own example, of the weakest readers in junior schools. We might "organise the service" better by looking at other countries, to see how they have managed things better. The Reading Recovery Project, for instance, developed in New Zealand by Professor Marie Clay, has belatedly been claimed by both Conservative and Labour parties as a possible response to our literacy problems. But it is very expensive and very time-consuming, and those who know about it warn strongly against it being seen as instant or cosmetic. It is very much a question of commitment: how serious are we ? how much are we prepared to spend ? We might, if we cared enough, spent enough, actually get these pupils better at reading - by spending money in an intelligent way.

There is money available, for NCC booklets and SEAC bulletins, and other favoured causes. In 1990, more money was spent on setting up one City Technology College, than was spent on National Curriculum work in schools for the whole school population, throughout the country. "Put your money where your mouth is" we say, when we doubt someone's honesty. By that standard, the National Curriculum is a great deal of mouth, and not much money.

# CHAPTER SIX: Marked for Life ?

## ASSESSMENT

I remember being assessed. I remember junior school, when they put up lists for term marks, and exam marks, and the top of each list got a prize. I remember spelling tests; ten questions, one mark for each. I had piano lessons for a year, but I never got further than grade one. I passed six O levels and failed two, and was made a prefect. I went to university, got a prize for writing an essay, and got a degree - like almost everyone else. After an interview, I got a job, and two years later I passed my driving test.

There's nothing very special about that career. Everyone could do their own, and it might be better or worse than mine, but it would have that mixture there - objective and subjective, specific test and general examination, common achievement and competitive award.

We need to have that background in mind, because our ideas don't just drop out of the sky. What seems like "human nature" or "common sense" may be a particular piece of past experience, or a generalisation based on specific, very limited knowledge.

I begin in this basic, cautious manner because assessment, like other educational issues, is complex. People try to simplify it, which is understandable, but can be very dangerous. With the results of testing, for instance, there are clear risks of misinterpretation, that league tables and simple scores will suggest quality or superiority which may not exist. Consequently there is a movement within education to take more factors into account, to try to to produce a more sophisticated picture of what is going on. Can we look at, not just the scores pupils achieve, but the difference school makes to their achievements between two dates ? How does what they end up with compare with what they came in with ?

This is called the "value-added" approach, and it's a promising, if complicated development. Kenneth Clarke, as Education Minister, described it as "cooking the figures."

Vocabulary matters. Words are not as simple as they look, particularly if they happen to be loaded. What does "standards" mean ? It might mean levels of attainment, how good the pupils are; or it might mean criteria, the ways by which we judge how good the pupils are. So, if the pupils get good marks, that could be because the tests are too easy; in other words, (loaded words), standards are high because the standards are too low. You have to be careful to say what you mean.

We make assumptions about assessment. "Five foot, eleven and a half inches" is more exact than "Fairly tall", so we assume that numbers are more precise than words. Sometimes they are. "67%" probably says more than "a fair effort" - particularly if other marks are available. But what about this ?

"C. This is a lively story, although I think you've rushed the ending. Next time, try to get closer to the people in your story."

Here the words say more than the grade. They identify a quality ('lively'), make a criticism (hurried ending), and suggest a target for future work (more detailed attention to character). All these provide more information than the stark grade C - although at GCSE level that grade could be the decisive factor in getting a job or a place at college.

That doesn't mean the grade is wrong. It means we have to be clear about the purposes of assessment. If it is necessary to put candidates in a rank order (as it may be, say, for university entrance) then grading will be useful; for day-to-day school work that may be a distraction. Research suggests that when pupils are given a mark and a comment they pay more attention to the mark, even though the comment may be more important in directing their attention to future avenues for improvement. "Where am I ?"is a different question from "How do I get better ?", and will therefore have a different answer.

Nobody ever got heavier by being weighed, and there needs to be an intelligent, considered relationship between teaching and testing. For the Government to create two separate bodies (NCC and SEAC) to oversee those two functions was always a risk. John Major's comments indicate that he sees "testing" as a limited, negative activity:
"Testing must not dominate the classroom. It must not swamp schools in paperwork. Nor should it be driven by too theoretical an approach. We need to shift the emphasis towards shorter standardised tests, which the whole class can take at one time." But we also need to ask why. What precisely will these tests achieve ? What information are we after, and what use do we intend to make of it ? And to answer these questions must be a theoretical activity, in the sense that it must have a theory behind it. When Major demands "shorter, standardised

tests" he does not want to get involved in discussion, but he is valuing simplicity, speed, convenience. We have to ask, are these criteria sufficient ?

There's teaching, and there's testing, and the links between the two are powerful and subtle. The main weakness of this National Curriculum is that it was conceived as a test: the primary, urgent aim was to produce results, compile league tables, rather than teach anything. As a result the curriculum was defined in terms of attainment levels rather than knowledge or skills. A genuinely educational approach would have centred first on "what is to be taught", and only then looked at "how is it to be assessed ?"

Assessment has become more complicated, but not only in school. Businesses do not simply calculate their success by counting this year's profits; they look at investment, research and development, long-term trends, future markets, their impact on the environment. You might try to guess at a manager's skill by looking at their salary and counting the hours that they work; but an intelligent firm would also look at their role within the organisation, their effect on others, the work that they enable to take place. IBM, for example, assess their managers by looking at quality of work, customer satisfaction and the morale of employees below the manager. How would Education Ministers fare, judged on those criteria ?

We have to resist the urge to simplify, the confident assumption that "it's only x", "or "it's just a matter of y." Assessment is a complicated process, with many different possibilities, not a single operation. Some assessment will be short, or simple , or convenient, but only if we choose to make it that way. It all depends on what you want to assess, and for what reason.

Let's imagine that you were carrying out a historical comparison, between the manual dexterity of teenagers - 1890 compared with 1990. How would you test that ? "Use of computers" would come up with one result, and "manipulation of wing collars" with another. Girls would perform differently from boys, and money, social class, past experience would all have an effect.

That may seem a silly example. Surely there are clear touchstones, simple educational jobs that everyone does - like number tables, or spelling. Tables are useful for everyday calculation, and I think children ought to know them. They were a dominant part of my own early maths education, but for some children now they compete with other issues - estimation, for instance. We were never taught about estimation, never encouraged to value or think about the intelligent guess. But if the test is "tables only" then pupils who have done tables and estimation may be at a disadvantage against those who have done only tables.

It might be right to do tables only. But in that case, the issues have to be discussed and agreed, before the test is chosen. We get a lot of headlines based on the results of inappropriate testing, but we shan't get a clear picture of achievement unless the testing is based on the same assumptions as the teaching, and that takes time and thought.

What about spelling ? Here again, this was a dominant part of my own early education, and I was lucky in being able to spell well. (I do think it was luck. I didn't work hard at it, and I do know others who went through exactly the same education, suffered embarrassment and worse for their failure, desperately wanted to be able to spell - but still can't do so). "A list of spellings", it is argued, will sort out who can spell and who can not.

Well, it may do. But there are people who can spell for a test, who will then get the same word wrong in their normal writing. There are mechanical enthusiasts who can spell "carburettor" but not "friend". Perhaps we should test the spelling of pupils' 'normal' writing, rather than words we have imposed upon them ? But then some pupils' normal writing will include words like "surreptitious", while canny mistake-avoiders will write "The cat sat on the mat" and sit back, knowing they have made no errors.

You might set out a list of ten words, in order of difficulty. How about -
fat
fill
film
friend
fulfil
famine
future
ferocious
fallacious
facetious

If you can spell 'fat' you get level 1, if you can spell them all you get level 10. Simple, isn't it ?

But then the doubts come in. Spelling isn't simply a question of

69

complication. We'd all agree that "facetious" is harder than "fat", but is "famine" harder than "fulfil" ? How do we decide ? Is it rarity value, or the possibility of confusion - fullfil, fullfill, fulfill and so on. Nothing, in this area, should be taken for granted.

## ASSESSMENT IN THE NATIONAL CURRICULUM

Assessment was always a key part of the National Curriculum, with tests at 7, 11, 14 and 16 an integral part of the Education Reform Act. The political case was that parents would now have a clear view of how their children were doing, but the reality was much more complex than that. "From Policy to Practice" agreed with the Task Group that "Assessment is at the heart of the process of promoting children's learning" (6.1) , and went on to identify five purposes which that assessment would serve:

"Formative - information to help teachers plan

Summative - evidence of achievement evaluative - in identifying areas where there might need to be further effort, resources or curriculum change

Informative - for parents; but also for governors, LEAs and the wider community;

Professional development - enabling teachers to reflect on their work and gain access to new thinking.(6.2)"

That's an ambitious package, and rightly a complex one. Whatever the pressures of time and publicity, this is a matter which requires careful thought and precision.

In setting up its assessment arrangements, the National Curriculum settled early on for the idea of ten levels. It is not clear where this came from, or why this was seen as the best approach. It was provided by the task group on Assessment, who were answering very specific questions posed by Kenneth Baker. Since then, a lot of ring binder files have floated under the bridge, and most of the task group's work has been forgotten. Somehow, obstinately, the ten levels remain.

They were not based on what teachers were doing. "From Policy to Practice" does mention this possibility, claiming that "The introduction for the first time of a national assessment system.....presents a major opportunity for taking forward some of the good practice that has been developed by schools and LEAs, and as part of the new approach offered by G.C.S.E." (6.l)

But that's not what happened. There are many interesting developments in assessment - checklists, comment banks, pupil self-assessment, related modules, coursework, mid-task review, target-setting and so on. To my knowledge no school was running a ten-level system. What is so special about the ten levels that means we have to use them ?

The idea is this. Working groups divide their subject area into attainment targets, and then try to fix ten levels of attainment within each target. These are given written descriptions, so that a teacher sees what a pupil has done, and then seeks to find the description which best fits the work.

You can imagine some problems straight away. What happens if the work doesn't match any of the descriptions ? What happens if it seems to fall between them, or matches a bit of one and a bit of another ? We need to look at some examples.

ENGLISH: In the writing profile component, dealing with knowledge about language, pupils should be able to:
level 7  Comment on examples of appropriate and inappropriate use of language in written texts, with respect to purpose, topic and audience.
level 8 Demonstrate some knowledge of organisational differences between spoken and written English.
level 9 Demonstrate some knowledge of ways in which language varies between different types of written text e.g. personal letter, formal letter, printed instructions, newspaper report, play script.

You will notice that these are not different ways of doing the same thing, with level 9 'better' than level 7.  They are actually different things, and you could argue that bits of level 9 are easier than bits of level 7.

It all depends what you mean by "demonstrate some knowledge of..." How much knowledge ? Demonstrate it how ? By repeating a teacher statement learnt by heart ? By writing correct answers in a timed examination ? By writing samples which actually show differences between types of text, without defining what those differences are ?

This is not nit-picking. This is an attempt to clarify confusion, which has been brought about by this pattern of assessment. The ten levels and the lists of statements look precise, a clear ladder up which pupils will ascend, a rung at a time.

But the ladder is not clear. Some of the rungs are better defined than others, and there is not confident agreement about their place on the ladder, or whether there actually is a ladder at all.

By training, I am an English teacher. I think English has an excellent pattern of assessment (G.C.S.E. coursework), but English may be a special case, and is sometimes viewed by other disciplines as a subjective minefield. We should look at another example, something with real content, and an objective method. Like Science.

Under attainment target 2 (Life and living processes) pupils at level 8 should - among other things -
"understand that the impact of human activity on the Earth is related to the size of the population, economic factors and industrial requirements."
Got that ? (You're right. It isn't easy).
Those at level 10, meanwhile, should - among other things -
"make informed judgements about some of the major ecological issues facing society."

Now, who defines this hierarchy, and on what basis ? Do science teachers all agree that those who "make informed judgements..." are superior scientists to those who "understand that the impact.." ? Is the latter a necessary requirement before tackling the former ? Or is there perhaps a hope that political debate about ecological issues should be postponed until the very end of the process, reserved only for those who "understand that the impact of human activity on the Earth is related to ..."

There is a different, crucial objection. These descriptions are not of pupil activity, but of subject content. Whether or not they have the stages right, these sentences describe "issues to be tackled" rather than "characteristics of pupils' work." So they may guide teachers about what to do next, but they do not offer much help in discriminating between the performances of different pupils.

It is hard to envisage a science teacher organising a class in which some pupils were pursuing level 8 while some pursued level 10. For the moment, let us suppose that the aim is to approach level 8 with as many members of the class as possible. The teacher produces a range of factual material - videos, text books, newspaper cuttings - which potentially inform pupils about population, economic factors and industrial requirements. How do they then decide which pupils have, and which have not, "understood" that the impact of human activity is related to these things ?

Here are some possibilities:

(a) A typed sheet:
"The impact of human activity on the Earth is related to the size of the population, economic factors and industrial requirements." TRUE or FALSE. Pupils underline which answer they think is correct.

(b) A test a week later.
"Complete the following sentence:"The impact of human activity on the Earth is related to i.................ii...................iii.................."

(c) An essay.
"Which are the key factors influencing human activity on Earth ?"Support your answer with specific illustrations.

(d)A group assignment.
"Your group's job is to produce a TV documentary about Humans on Earth. It should deal with the most important influences on human activity."

(e) An individual interview, after access to information.Teacher asks pupil:
"What have you learnt about human activity on Earth ?"

It doesn't matter which of these you prefer. The point is that it would not be simple to decide, pupil by pupil, who had "understood" this, and it is very likely that each of these testing methods would produce different results. It is probable that some pupils would 'pass' on some tests but not on others; there would not even be a consistent rank order between them. So a teacher's choice of task could actually decide who was at which level.

And that's just one subject. Other subjects are different, present different problems - and have been tackled differently. This means that while the statements of attainment for Science are often concerned with content, for Technology they are content-free. They could apply to a pupil solving a problem through the use of wood, or cardboard, or plastic; they might be designing a toothbrush, a block of flats or a spacecraft. It also means that some of the statements sound a bit vague, and are hard to match against pupil performance.

Jim Sweetman, in an article on Technology, points to a key problem with assessment:

"At level 4, children who are being expected to master the sporadic use of the full stop in their English stories are expected to "record ideas as they develop", "provide written justification" for their actions, and show success in "appraising results in relation to intentions." "(The Guardian 23.6.92)

This dramatically shows the inadequacy of the subject-based approach. We need subjects, but we need something more than subjects, to maintain an overview. Just as a timetable requires some central decisions about the allocation of time, so a universal system of assessment requires connections between the different elements. It should be somebody's job to make sure that the demands made by different subjects at level 4 are within reasonable proximity of each other, but this necessary, difficult task was not even attempted.

We are dealing here with complex issues, and the ways in which pupils work are also complex. Trying to simplify this into a clear pattern runs the risk of distorting the work. I am not going to offer a foolproof attainment target, or a surefire way of assessing a particular target; what I am offering is the strong gut feeling that the National Curriculum pattern is too cumbersome and too far removed from the actual school world of tasks and pupil work.

To provide the examples above, I have had to select. For Science, there are now 178 statements of attainment. Some of them are harder to take in than the two I have quoted above.

For this system to work a Science teacher has to be familiar with all these statements, so as to place each child's work at some point on the ladder (or ladders, since there are now four attainment targets for Science). That means a regular mental journey, away from the pupil performance, towards the grid, looking for the right description. Teacher effort and time goes on skimming through the descriptions, rather than looking exactly at what the child has or has not done.

That is personally frustrating for the teacher, because it feels like paperwork rather than teaching, but it is not even good assessment, because the energy is going on "can I find it somewhere ?" rather than "what is it they have done ?"

We need a pattern of assessment where the thought and energy goes into looking at the work, not the paperwork. I think we have such a pattern, in the GCSE, and that is where I think the National Curriculum should have gone in looking for its model.

## G.C.S.E.

Superficially, they look the same. The GCSE has levels, but only seven. They also have grade descriptions, verbal accounts of the kind of work you would expect to find in particular grades. But these are not the sole basis of the assessment, and I suspect they are retrospective, rationalisations of decisions already made.

I remember two Art teachers, agonising over a piece of coursework. I asked the source of their dilemma. One of them replied "Would you say this shows a simple understanding, or a basic understanding ?"

It's a verbal quibble, a desperate hunt for words which will indicate that a grade F piece is better than a grade G piece. You don't resolve it by saying the work is basic, but by looking at work which is worth a grade F, and at work which isn't. It is, literally, about drawing the line.

And that process, of discrimination and judgement, has at some point to be communal. Experienced assessors will skim through a pile of folders and allocate grades correctly, but only because they they have done that job before, and with others.

Assessment makes use of instinct, but instinct trained through discussion, supported by evidence. By marking with others, I learn about my own prejudices and strengths, and grasp the full range of the criteria being used. Trial markings and moderation gradually help me, and others with me, to know what a grade C looks like.

Remember Mill ? "The whole strength and value, then, of human judgement, depending on the one property, that it can be set right when it is wrong, reliance can be placed on it only when the means of setting it right are kept constantly at hand..."

This is true of teachers, and of examiners, whose task it is to define this year's grade C so that it is the same as last year's grade C - whether in Norfolk or Somerset. The system is not perfect, but it works as well as any other, and better than most. Dewy-eyed nostalgia for the good old days of 'O' level rigour is not supported by those who were close to the process. But the strength of GCSE assessment is in groupwork, not paperwork.

National Curriculum does not yet have that strength, although some have tried to put it there. The Task Group set up to advise on NC assessment recommended regular marking meetings, at which teachers of various subjects would meet to compare the levels of their marking. That means teachers, sat round a table, looking at work from a range of pupils and coming to agreement about how it should be marked.

G.C.S.E. experience suggests that this is also a marvellous way of training teachers, of helping them become more aware of what they are doing, and of pooling the benefits of their varied experience. It is, however, expensive. It takes time, and it can't be squeezed in after school. You have to pay teachers to work in this way, which means either covering their classes with supply teachers, or allocating more teachers to schools so that on a regular basis some teachers are involved in moderation rather than teaching.

This is not a price the government is prepared to pay. It would be expensive, but the refusal to pay it is also a decision to settle for second-rate assessment, the paperwork without the groupwork, the levels without the thought.

I keep saying this is a complicated job, and it is interesting to see what happens to people who tackle it. SEAC was created specifically to carry out the government's wishes on assessment. This was an appointed body contrived to resist the progressive tendencies of the education lobby, and set proper standards.

And what happened ? As SEAC became drawn into the actual process, looked more carefully and clearly at what was going on, so they became more sympathetic to what schools were trying to do, and less happy with the party line. They were not drugged, bribed or seduced; they were persuaded, by experience, and only by a brutal change of leadership (accompanied by important resignations) could SEAC be kept loyal to its partisan brief.

At teacher level, the results of such contortion can look very strange. I teach a year 9 English group, for whom I shall have to provide levels of attainment. This is how I am to reach the writing level:

First determine the constituent AT levels, based on the NC Test levels and the TA level in the case of AT4/5:-

If the TA in AT4/5 is at level 7, and the NC Test level for AT3 (Writing) is at level 8, then the PC level is the AT3 NC Test level.-

if the TA in 4/5 is not at level 7, but is higher than level 4, then the PC level is worked out as follows:
AT3 NC test level x 8  PLUS  AT4/5 TA level x 2;
Divide this total by 10.-

if the NC Test level for ATs 4 and 5 is at or below level 4, the PC level is worked out as follows:
AT3 NC Test level x 8 plus AT4 NC test level plus AT5 NC Test level.
Divide THIS TOTAL by 10.

Everything clear now ?

IDEOLOGICAL WARFARE

Assessment is the core of this political operation. Assessment is about control, value and expense. Assessment says how we are doing and what has been done, so it is vital for the various factions that they should get their way over assessment.

The battle over the testing of seven-year olds has been a graphic illustration of this. Kenneth Baker, under pressure from the Conservative right wing, offered this manifesto:"I am determined that tests will meet parents' expectations, that they will be rigorous, and will test children's knowledge and understanding as well as skills."

We are, don't forget, talking about seven-year olds. But this has nothing to do with parents' expectations; it is a matter of political symbols, flying the right educational flags - rigour, understanding, knowledge. Precisely what these mean in the context of testing seven-year olds is a different question, but not one that politicians have to resolve.

When SEAC awarded a contract for testing to a particular group whose methods were seen as progressive, Stuart Sexton (a former adviser to Keith Joseph), objected that this was at total variance with what the Prime Minister wanted, and would not test children's literacy and numeracy against national averages. Now, why should it be so important to keep the Prime Minister happy ? Aren't we simply after the method of testing that gives us the most useful results?

Dr. Sheila Lawlor, of the Centre for Policy Studies, commented as follows:
"All of this is a game devised by education theorists, but it will be at the expense of what children are at school to do. It is absolutely crackers."

Note the matey playground language, with its cheery assumption that the other side aren't using their brains at all. This has become a popular ministerial trademark - "cranky...dotty theories." The image of the game, though, is accurate. Different sides, keen on winning, measuring their success like a tug of war - how far towards our ideal has the handkerchief moved ? Will another tug, a bit more muscle, get us the result we want ?

Now the key players are impatient. After years of confident government statements about the quality of GCSE and its evidence of rising standards, Kenneth Clarke and John Major became disenchanted with coursework. In its place they would put the quick written test - simple, rapid and cheap.

It is interesting to see this process at work. This is how the SEAC recorder describes it:
"In July, the Prime Minister said he wanted GCSE to become a predominantly external examination. The Education Secretary followed this up by asking SEAC to advise how the coursework element in GCSE might most effectively be controlled and restrained. SEAC has suggested that..."
(SEAC recorder, no. 9 page 10)

Here it comes, down the line. The Prime Minister says..the Education Secretary follows...SEAC suggests... But where does it come from ? What is the thinking, the experience, the evidence which underlies the decision in the first place? Where did the Prime Minister get his ideas ? I think we should be told.

At present, and it is a volatile present where much could change, it is likely that short, external tests will be imposed over much of the curriculum. The strength of GCSE coursework was that it met two conflicting demands:
(a) that assessment tasks should be related to the content of teaching,

AND
(b) that criteria for assessment should be standardised across the country.

It did this by encouraging teachers to set their own tasks, but also committing them to a series of stages of communal assessment and moderation to ensure consistent standards.

The new tests, with some originality, reverse this pattern. The tests are set externally, running the risk that they will not relate to the actual work done, but they are then to be marked by the class teachers, creating the danger that scripts in different schools, or different parts of the country, will be marked differently. It is not a promising model.

The damage done by the "short, simple test" is considerable. I do not mean the distress, the unfairness and the important issues that the test will miss out, nor even the inevitable subsequent debate about whether the test was reliable or fair. The real danger is in the impact on teaching. The dry runs, past papers and endless rehearsals, which will themselves provide a powerful negative lesson of what learning is about. Past teachers of the 11-plus and of O level English Language do not look back to a heady time of flourishing standards; they remember boredom, repetition, narrow calculation. If, on top of that, the results of these "short, sharp tests" are to feed league tables which in turn decide pupil numbers, resources for schools and teaching jobs, we are in for a very grim time indeed.

This kind of testing, in fact, takes us away from the National Curriculum. A huge edifice like this cannot be tested in a simple, rapid way; parts of it, indeed (the English programmes of study, for instance) were defined with coursework in mind. If there is an arbitrary decision to reduce coursework, then logically there should also be a redefinition of "what English is." (Since these words were written, we have had the opening shots of this campaign, as the NCC - with a bit of help from its government masters - decided in September 1992 that English teaching needed to be reviewed). Presumably any part of this National Curriculum is also vulnerable to the same kind of sweeping, arbitrary revision.

The implications of simple testing for the NC as a whole are very interesting indeed. For if you have a simple test (which is quick and cheap to mark, because you get the teachers to do it as homework), you end up with a range of marks and pupils separated into a list. The marks of the test will split them, into a rank order. And if the test does that, why do you then need statements of attainment ?

There are already signs of a change of heart, or weakening resolve. Art, Music and PE, at the back of the assessment queue as of all others, will not now have statements of attainment at the ten levels. The reason for this, according to the National Curriculum Council, is that

"the working groups have not been able to define sufficiently persuasive differences between levels. All too often distinctions between levels are dependent upon unhelpfully subtle gradations between adjectives; between 'simple' and 'more sophisticated', for example." (Additional Advice NCC Jan.92,C2)

I think that's a fair point, but it's not confined to Art, Music and PE. According to the NCC, these subjects are different from others:

"Assessment should not be unduly onerous, given the flexible nature of these subjects and the fact that primary teachers are required to teach a further six subjects over and above art, music and physical education. It cannot be in primary teachers' interests to have, as the Working Groups proposed, a total of 186 non-statutory statements in art, music and physical education, as well as the 60 statutory end of key stage statements." (C 4)

Primary teachers will be relieved to see such concern, but it comes a bit late in the day. What, you are tempted to ask, would be a reasonable load of statements for primary teachers to deal with ? Is it "in their interests" to have the burdens already imposed on them by English, Maths, Science, Technology, Geography and History ? And what is suddenly so special about the three at the end of the queue? You've heard it before:

"The flexible nature of art, music and physical education, in contrast to the other foundation subjects, renders the 10-level framework unduly restricting." (C 5)

It may be true. It would certainly be worth testing, through some consumer research. Are teachers of the six non-flexible subjects convinced that all their statements persuasively define differences between levels ? Do they find it in their interests to have their present number of statements of attainment, or do they too see some 'flexibility' in the subjects they teach ?

This question is not being seriously pursued - yet. Nobody is worried whether teachers are happy with what the law requires, and the teachers have become accustomed to operating systems about which they have not been consulted. In time, however, someone must address the question - is this the best we can do ?

Meanwhile I offer a personal, subjective impression. Over the last ten years I have been involved in a range of innovations related to assessment - coursework, oral work, CPVE and Records of Achievement. Each of those has had their problems, their grey areas which concerned honest practitioners, but in each of them I have seen some teachers grasp new ideas with enthusiasm, and sometimes with surprise - that something which seemed alien or complicated could in fact be made to work. So far, I know of no teacher who has responded in this way to the assessment of the National Curriculum.

The present apparatus - of statements at ten levels - was created to provide a framework for teacher assessment. The current government message, however, is that teacher assessment is not to be trusted. Where there is a choice between teacher marks and test marks, tests will decide.

In the summer of 1991 I went to a conference about NC assessment. A large audience of anxious teachers was addressed by a series of experts, among them an official responsible for the quality audit for Key Stage 3. I witnessed this chilling exchange:
TEACHER: Am I right in thinking that in all cases the SAT will override the teacher assessment, if they don't agree ?
OFFICIAL: You are.
TEACHER: And there is no right of appeal ?
OFFICIAL: That is correct.
TEACHER: In which case, why am I making the teacher assessment?
OFFICIAL: Good question.

There is a deep lack of trust here in personal judgement, and professional skill. This is balanced by a touching faith in the accumulation of unrelated fragments. If we can only make the bits small enough, and then add them up, perhaps we shall get reliable assessment. It doesn't actually work that way, and there is research to prove it, but the research is part of a thinking, rational world whose values are rejected.

If we are back to crude assertion and simple tests, then everybody has wasted a lot of time on a very complicated system. Do we try to perfect it, fiddling here and there to improve the machinery ? Do we hope for some radical reform, when education is one day run by someone with vision, energy and guts ?

Or do we simply leave it in place, because it was a part of the package that Kenneth Baker rushed through Parliament ?

I think assessment is too important, too interesting, to be left to the politicians, but we shall not end up with a better pattern of assessment until we have removed some of the debris from the very recent past. It cannot be healthy for teachers to be operating a complex, time-consuming apparatus in which they do not believe; this particular section of the bright new edifice is an instant slum.

# CHAPTER SEVEN: Keep The Customer Satisfied

EDUCATION FOR CONSUMERS ?

Throughout the development of the Education Reform Act, there persists the image of the market: something is on offer, and the customer is entitled to the best they can possibly get at the cheapest possible price. To do this they need to know what they are looking at, they should have the freedom to complain, and the ultimate freedom of being able to go elsewhere. When all these conditions are met, the image suggests, we shall have quality education.

As with all images, we have to test whether the picture fits. Education is not a simple product, like baked beans, to be passed across the counter. Talk of "delivering" the curriculum implies a bottle of milk, to be simply picked up and put on the doorstep. We know what a bottle of milk should contain; there is not that agreement about what education should contain.

It is not simply a question of ingredients. Most views of education see it as a process. Pupils are not simply told things, or made to learn them. They change during the process, not only in what they know, but in what they can do, what they are aware of and in the way they think. And in our tradition, it is also argued that they develop attitudes and values which will affect their whole lives as adults. That is a more ambitious claim, which makes the business of education much subtler than a simple cash transaction.

There is a further problem. Who are the customers ? Much of the ERA rhetoric appeals to parents, whose money funds the process. They have been cheated by the professionals, it is alleged, deprived of choice and bemused by jargon. Only by taking power away from the producers and restoring it to the consumers will we get true quality.

But the consumers are actually the children. It is they who 'get' the service, and they who are supposed to benefit from it. This is not necessarily to venture into the murky world of pupil power, but it is one more reason for careful thought, that this whole issue is not as simple as some have made it seem.

Parents are concerned for their children, but they are not always the best judge of how they should be educated. Which exams pupils should be entered for, which method will best ensure their chances of reading, how technology should be tackled in a cross-curricular context - parents may well be interested in all these questions, but there is no reason why they should be equipped to solve them. And if they are empowered to tackle them, there is no reason why all parents should come up with the same answers. You cannot run a school by parental referendum.

Not, to be fair, that most of them would want it. The government seems to assume a state of constant warfare, but the parents I meet are interested, sometimes concerned, often grateful. There may be things they don't understand, or things they think I should know, but they aren't consumed by this permanent sense of grievance. There are not queues of them fighting to be governors, and the annual meeting to which they are now entitled, where they are encouraged to bring their complaints, is a very low key affair. Yet again legislation has ignored a complex, subtle reality and in its place has settled for the myth.

This is an argument for the place of expertise. It is not an argument that teachers are always right, that they cannot learn from contact with parents, or that parents should have no say in educational decisions. Like any teacher who has worked for closer links with parents, through meetings, publishing information, teaching sample lessons and answering enquiries, I recognise the benefits of this process, for me as well as for parents. The nature of that dialogue will vary: the occasion for it may be general background interest, or anxiety about a particular subject, confusion about media reports of current developments  or concern that an individual child should make the most of their talents. Any of those would be a good reason for teacher-parent dialogue, but each of them would make for a different form of contact.

With the Education Reform Act there is a third class of customer - future employers. Not all pupils will find jobs, even eventually, and not all education should be aimed at the workplace, but it is important that employers should understand what happens in schools, and if possible should support it. A further motive behind the National Curriculum was to set up courses in such a way that employers could have some influence over the content of education (through their membership of working groups for particular subjects). Once the curriculum was defined, it would be possible for them to see for themselves the skills and knowledge which pupils would acquire.

So, what does the National Curriculum mean to its customers?

# PUPILS

In some superficial ways there has been an immediate effect. Pupils of secondary age have had to get used to being in years 7 - 11 (rather than 1 - 5). Many primary children have experienced a drastic change to the pattern of their day as a testing season is introduced, and in summer 1993 all year nine pupils will have a two week period in which they will undergo a series of one-hour examinations.

"Pencil-and-paper tests" are not as quick as they look. They seem convenient and cheap, because formally they're over very quickly, but if a lot depends on them the canny teacher will ensure that pupils are ready for their particular demands. Thus an increasing number of the lessons before the tests will be devoted to spotting questions, framing model answers, calculating time to match the marking scheme. This trains pupils in test technique, but it also teaches them that education is about memory and prediction, short-term performance in an artificial game with elaborate rules. Already schools are asking for copies of model papers, setting up times of the year when pupils can sit mock tests, so as to get practice before the real thing. That may be what we want for our children, but as a parent I'd appreciate being asked first, and as a teacher I can see a lot of lessons becoming narrowly aimed, repetitive and dull.

That's the gloomy side. To be more positive, a clear curriculum should give pupils some sense of where they are going, a view of the road ahead. This may be the case for a determined few, but the bulk and language of the National Curriculum documents are not such as to inspire the run of school pupils.

At the lower reaches of the ability range, this could be very sad. " But miss, I do have some understanding of..." Do they or don't they ? If you either tick it or you don't, it's a pass/fail exam, whatever the SEAC booklet says, and if you make pupils confront hurdles they want to get over them. Given the nebulous, verbal nature of many attainment targets, how do you explain to some pupils that they haven't attained them ? The rhetoric says that this is a recording of positive achievement, but that is not the way the attainments are defined.

There has been an uneasiness throughout about the relationship of National Curriculum to Records of Achievement (ROA). ROA was one of the few successful grass-roots movements in education, a determined campaign by teachers and others to make it possible for all pupils to celebrate their achievements. Two of its strengths are:

(1) It has an overall view, taking in individual subjects but not being confined by them, and also recognising achievement outside the classroom.

(2) It is a process of review in which pupils are themselves involved, through discussion, reflection and writing. Much of the assessment is in their words, and therefore makes sense to them.

Neither of these applies to the National Curriculum. That is a vast, wordy apparatus which celebrates the narrowly academic virtues, and with current developments is likely to move even further in that direction. One certain result of this will be to disqualify large numbers of pupils from feeling that they can be successful. That may be part of the aim; some value a system which is so fiercely selective that it turns the majority of pupils into failures, but that was hardly what was envisaged in "From Policy to Practice."

This is not simply a plea for the less able. They are likely to be among the most severe casualties, but they are not the only ones. All pupils benefit from being given a clear view of their work, and with the National Curriculum that can be difficult to provide.

The strength of ROA has been to encourage pupils to gain a clearer view of their own work - through the efforts of teachers as well as those of the pupils themselves. I watched a trampoline lesson recently where each member of the group took their turn on the trampoline, but at key moments other members of the group were invited to analyse what was happening:
"Why is she finding that hard ? What does she need to do ?...stretch her arms out...Hips; turn the hips over..."

This was careful, precise analysis. In the corner was a video camera, filming each pupil, so that when they had finished their turn they could look at themselves in action, get a clear picture of their own movements and position. In this way, each pupil could get clear feedback about their own performance, and identify precisely what they needed to do next.

That seems to me a healthy example of self-assessment. Its main purpose is improvement, the student's understanding of their own learning, and the allocation of letter grades or rank orders would get in the way.

Compare that with this sheet, designed for Technology self-assessment in year 10:

Attainment descriptions:
You have:
1. asked straightforward questions (with some help)
2. asked questions which have helped you identify a need which
needs a solution
3. used information about people, materials and ways of making things looked at
earlier times in history and at other parts of the world
4. devised ways of finding non-printed information    looked at the need from
other people's points of view

and so on, to

10. discovered and understood people's needs, and their feelings about them, in
several different situations.

This is not, to be fair, required by the NC. But it is very obviously
influenced by it. Someone has taken a positive teaching idea - pupil self-
assessment - and then tried to fit it to what they see as the official model
(attainment statements, arranged in ten levels). Pupils who are handed this sheet
are being taught that assessment is not about looking at your work, it's about
finding a predetermined comment on a list of ten. That might be something you
require of teachers, but as a strategy for pupils it is misguided, to say the least. It
would not have happened, though, without the National Curriculum.

Pupils should assess themselves, but not in this way. They should reflect
on their work, and try to be clear about what they have achieved and which
problems they have overcome. They should seek to identify difficulties they have
encountered, and future targets for their subsequent work. That is the continuum
within which they will progress, and it is one in which - as records of
achievement have demonstrated - pupils of widely differing abilities can achieve
a positive, detailed analysis of their work. To teach them that all skills and
knowledge come in ten-level hierarchies is, by comparison, a waste of time.

What do  they make of it? This is a year 8 pupil, talking about Maths :
"We all do the level 5 test, and if we do well we do the level 6. Those
who don't do very well do the level 4. "

"From Policy to Practice" described a different pattern, in which
attainment targets and programmes of study
"allow for, and encourage, progression whilst also accommodating

87

differentiation. The 10 levels of attainment for each subject are designed to enable teachers, pupils and their parents to be clear about what is expected next of each pupil, and pupils to make identifiable progress through the levels at their own pace and from their own starting point." (4.15)

It's an attractive ideal, but it's not happening. Very often, as we have seen, the difference between levels is not a difference in quality, but in content. Level 8 is about a different topic from level 7, and in terms of resources that makes it harder for pupils in the same class to be tackling different levels. And the load for the teacher in making any assessment at all is substantial, so that to be testing different levels simultaneously is almost impossible.

"Accommodating differentiation" is an ideal. When pupils are bored, it is often because every member of a class is being required to tackle the same task, and the boredom may stem from the task being too difficult, or too easy. But this class teaching, with everyone doing the same thing, does not derive from some teacherly conviction that all pupils are the same. It comes partly from economics, that in most schools we are required to teach 25 pupils at a time, and partly from the logistical problems of organising various activities simultaneously - problems which tend to increase as the pupils get older and the subject matter becomes more sophisticated.

Differentiation is possible. It is not easy, and it is not widely practised, but it can be done. When it is done, it involves careful advance planning, and a limitation of the core, the work that everyone does. Most teachers expect the whole class to do a number of tasks, and may then tack on some extras for the brightest, or those who cannot cope, or those who finish first. In a differentiated classroom, there is less " work that everyone must do", and more time devoted to "different people doing different things." By defining a massive core, a body of work which all pupils should tackle, the National Curriculum makes it less likely that differentiation will take place.

Few pupils will make much sense of NC, although it may appeal to the sharp and lazy, who will be able to identify level 10 statements of attainment which do not require the preceding effort of levels 8 and 9. For the ablest and most creative pupils, however, it offers little incentive.

The National Curriculum is inert. It is already known and defined, written down in print. If an able pupil comes up with an astonishing piece of originality - as they do - this may well be denied NC recognition, because it has not been anticipated. The whole apparatus implies that we already know the territory, we can say in advance what the best work will look like, and although that may be true for much of the learning that goes on, it will not be true for all of it. This difficult area, of originality and innovation, is one that is precious to many of our best pupils, and for them to sense that such contributions are not properly valued - because they're not in the documents - would be a serious impoverishment. Education is about growth, the exploration of new areas, and the suggestion that we know it all already will kill the process dead.

## PARENTS AND EMPLOYERS

Many of the reservations concerning pupils also affect parents and employers. The best test is a simple one - do you know adults who have read NC literature and understood it ? There is a busy minor industry of explaining it all, through newspapers, television and separate publications, some of it very patient and well-meaning, but to the majority of adults in this country the National Curriculum is a blur, a nice idea whose details they do not understand.

And if they are uncertain of the outline, to expect them to understand the assessments is something else again. The intention was to provide clear future targets which pupils and parents would understand, but look again at how they're written. This is the attainment statement for one level of one mathematical attainment target. You've either got there or you haven't:

"Pupils should
(a) use an appropriate non-calculator method to multiply or divide two numbers.
(b) Find fractions or percentages of quantities.
(c) Refine estimations by 'trial and improvement methods'.
(d) Use units in context."

So when they tell you that your child is at level 5 for Attainment Target 2 (Number), how much wiser are you ? Not at all, unless you go back and read through the literature, and even then there's a lot of sorting out to do. Maybe your child has mastered three of these but not the other, maybe they use units in some contexts but not others, maybe the teacher is not sure whether their "non-calculator" method is actually "appropriate".

And now there is the further complication, that the "teacher assessment level" may be different from the "standardised attainment level." You will get the SAT level, because that is your legal right, but you are also legally entitled to go to the school to demand the teacher assessment level at any time, and within two weeks they must tell you what it is. But if it may later be over-ridden by the SAT level, why should you bother ?

The appeal throughout has been to parents, over the heads of teachers. "You haven't been given a clear picture,but now we'll make sure you get it" is the implied message, but if that is the promise it has not yet been kept. Reporting to parents on the progress of their children is not a simple matter.
Complete the following sentence:
"As a parent, what I really want to know is -

- will she pass her exams ?
- is she happy ?
- what will she do when she leaves ?
- is she behaving ?
- what is her homework about ?
- is she working as hard as she could ?
- how does she compare with her class ?
- what does she need to work on
- how does she compare with the national average ?
- what can I do to help her ?

Parents have never agreed on "what they want to know", and as a teacher I have encountered each of the above. Some parents want the chance to see an exercise book, or a list of marks, or a rank order, or a report with suggestions for future work. Some prefer the chance to talk face to face, to hear what teachers have to say and then ask questions; some prefer this process to be carried out while their children are there, while others strongly insist on their absence. There isn't a party line or a standard practice, and some parents would be very upset if there were.

The official view of the National Curriculum, however, offers a simple guarantee:
"This combination of clear targets and national tests will help ensure that...you, as a parent, can hold your child's school to account for the progress your child is making and for the standards of the school generally."
(Your Child and the NC, DES 1991, p.3)

There's a combative tone there, which suggests that the school may seek to evade its responsibilities. This is reinforced on page 11, where parents are assured that

"The school must give you an annual report on your child's progress, showing how your child is progressing in the National Curriculum and other subjects. In the years when your child takes the national tests - at 7, 11, 14 and 16 - the report will give you the results."

So, you get test scores and a report on progress. How is that progress to be measured ?

"All children start at 5 years old working towards level 1, and are likely to move on by one level every two years."(p.11)

So does that mean a move of one level means that everything is all right ? A move of two levels indicates a brilliant school?These are, as the accompanying diagram admits, very rough averages for enormous variations in attainment.

The problem is that the government has inserted itself into the parent-teacher dialogue, creating an awkward, irregular triangle. This uneasy relationship is illustrated by "How Is Your Child Doing At School ?" - a parent's guide to tests and reports for 14 year olds. Part of this is explanation, on a very simple level:

"WHY TEST ?
We all want our children to achieve higher standards."

Well, yes, but will the tests produce the higher standards ? Would any tests produce higher standards ? (Why don't we just do tests, instead of teaching?) And will they tell us why the child is or isn't attaining them ? Those questions aren't answered. Instead, parents get a reassuring guide to the territory:

"Each National Curriculum subject has its own set of challenging targets which cover all aspects of the subject. Each target is divided into 10 steps, or levels of attainment, which steadily get more difficult as children get older."

You can almost hear the tone of voice, going slowly so the dim ones at the back will pick it up.

"Because attainment targets are always assessed against this same 10-level scale, it is possible to see what progress is made over time."

This is the key justification for 10-level attainment, that it offers parents a simple, consistent check on progress throughout the years of compulsory schooling.

But it doesn't. As we have seen, subjects are divided up into attainment targets, and attainment targets may themselves be complex, and the teacher assessment on an attainment target may not match the SAT attainment on the same target. None of that complexity is hinted at here. Instead, there's a nice little line drawing to show you what's required - a pupil's science paper in which the misspelling 'balence' has been obviously corrected. It's not the science that matters, but the spelling.

There is still the suggestion that the government needs to be concerned for standards because the schools aren't. Parents are reassured that

"..the school must tell you " certain detailed information,

and

"..the school may tell you:
the results in this Summer's National Curriculum tests of mathematics and science.

If it does not, you can ask for the results."

So there. Keep the blighters on their toes.

And it's not only teachers who may fall down on the job. Parents apparently require guidance as to how they should react to the results.

A series of shaded boxes are printed, giving levels and examples of attainment in maths and science, with a column indicating "WHAT THIS MEANS":
8: ..above what is expected of typical 16 year olds - this is therefore exceptional achievement for a 14 year old.
7: ..14 year olds achieving this level would be doing better than average for their age and should be capable of achieving a good GCSE result.
5/6: These are the levels expected of typical 14 year olds. But you will want to discuss with the teachers whether your son or daughter may be able to reach higher levels.

4 and below: ..You need to discuss with the teachers why your son or daughter is working at these levels. It could be that your son or daughter is not doing as well as he or she should. He or she may however have special educational needs. The Department's leaflet: Children with Special Needs gives more information about this."

It's ludicrous. They're generalising about a whole population, so there's not much to say but "Well done if you're good, if you're not pull your socks up - unless you're SEN." "He or she may however.." is just the tip of an iceberg of vagueness, reflecting the basic fact that they literally don't know what they're talking about. All they can offer is more copies of this or some other leaflet, but they keep saying that if you want anything precise, or specifically helpful, you have to come back to the teacher. (Who just happens to work in the same obstructive school that may be reluctant to hand over these priceless results).

"Your Child and the National Curriculum" came to the same lame conclusion. What do you do if you want more information ?

"You can find out more about what your child is doing and what the school can offer by: talking to your child's teacher at a parents' evening or open day."

And the Parent's Charter is the same. It accumulates a catalogue of dubious rights. Parents are assured that "you have the right to say which school you prefer" (but not the right to go there); "pupils can choose to drop art and music from age 14" (but they are not guaranteed the right to study both); and parents can appeal against the result of a public exam (but not, apparently, that of an NC test). In the end, though, it's "A Partnership with Your School", and "the best schools have always been guided by the principles of the Citizen's Charter." Well, who would have believed it ?

Nothing has changed. Most schools sent reports home, and most schools ran parents' evenings. The tests and levels are new, but they won't make sense on their own - and in some cases they may conflict with the evidence provided by the teacher. As a parent, what do you do then ?

The booklet talks as though the Government had invented the whole idea of teacher-parent contact, as though there needed to be legal compulsion for any reporting to take place at all. It proudly promises that parents can "ask to see National Curriculum documents at the school", but it's more likely that they will seek clarification from the teachers. In the end, it comes back to teachers, and for the National Curriculum to work the teachers will have to make it work.

Teachers can't be kept out of education, and at that point it matters what we say and how we say it. Already we have been put in difficult positions, having to issue option booklets which cannot describe the courses we will teach, introducing courses whose assessment has still not been decided. We may know what we think, but what on earth can we say ?

We have to be honest. Our obligation to our job, our pupils and ourselves will not be served by pretence, and if what we say does not match the government rhetoric or assumptions of the media, so be it. We have to acknowledge the legality of an elected government, and seek to carry out our obligations in a constructive fashion, but as professionals we also have to exercise our judgement. And I think that means explaining our situation and making clear the ways in which National Curriculum currently deters us from offering children the best education that we can provide. This is a delicate balance, and school management have a difficult, sensitive role in this respect, but simply keeping quiet is not enough.

At some point, the government rhetoric about parents must be supported - or denied - by actual parents. The image of the parent that emerges from the publicity is of a shadowy figure, vaguely drawn, ignorant and permanently distrustful of what the schools are doing. That may be an accurate picture, or a distortion, but that must be for parents to say.

This government has ignored professional opinion, and has paid scant attention to organised parental pressure groups. But in the long run they will have to take account of the wishes of parents, and how else are parents going to recognise the complexity of the situation unless teachers are prepared to tell them?

Whatever NC and its proponents imply, teachers are crucial, and the next chapter deals with the implications of NC for teachers in the classroom. First, though, a brief postscript on employers. Employers are no more a single party than pupils or parents - their views on schools, curriculum and reporting will be varied, although many of them will want information that is clear and can be rapidly digested. I doubt if many of them will become familiar with National Curriculum requirements, and many - like the parents - will ask for explanation from teachers.

Teachers and employers do in fact speak to each other quite often. Work experience placements are arranged, speakers invited, references supplied, and some teachers are seconded to work in industry. Many teachers know parents and former pupils who are active in the world of work, and there is not a total gulf of incomprehension between the two. Despite this, teachers are sometimes characterised - by members of the government among others - as economically innocent, divorced from the hard facts of industrial life, the real world where decisions are taken and money made.

But if any business embarked on a new venture in the way the government has launched the National Curriculum, they would be laughed out of the marketplace. The lack of advance planning, the ignorance of resources, the failure to consult, the squandering of money on inaccurate publicity, the making of speedy decisions which are broadcast and then expensively rescinded - all these symptoms of incompetence suggest an organisation sadly lacking in management skills. It would be hard to find a more striking example of how not to do business.

# CHAPTER EIGHT: The Teacher's Job

## UNDER ATTACK

"Stop knocking the teaching profession. You do not get the best from demoralised personnel."

That does not come from the Labour Party, or a teacher's union. It comes from the Conservative Political Centre group based in Poole, Dorset. They are advising Government leaders on future tactics, and this is the kind of thing they have in mind:

"I do not expect our teachers to return to rows of desks and the use of the blackboard, but there must be some purposeful education carried out in the happy chaos that has replaced them."

"The general standard of education in the places I used to go is no better than it was, and in some cases has probably diminished."

"Prince Charles' recent widely reported remarks expressing his dismay at low standards and low levels of achievement in education strike a strong chord in all of us."

"It has been the children of the average and below average ability who have been damaged by the leftwing advocacy of progressive teaching methods....."

These were all comments from Kenneth Clarke, at that time the Secretary of State for education. They were not supported by evidence but they were dismissive of the work of teachers. For him there was no question that the National Curriculum was a reaction to failure:

"..a response to ministers' fears in the early eighties that standards and content were not being upheld in schools."

Notice that it is <u>ministers</u>' fears which spark this off, and they see no need to check these against any professional analysis. Still, if the diagnosis is failure, who is responsible ?

Kenneth Clarke referred to educationalists with dotty theories, but that is no kind of answer. It is the teachers who work in the schools, and if the teachers have followed the theories, then they are the ones to blame. And they have been blamed, in varying ways but with consistent regularity. Government ministers have set the tone, but many others have been happy to join in. After all, we've all been to school, and we've all got little memories we're happy to avenge. Some of it was justified, and some of it wasn't, but teachers have come in for a lot of public criticism.

Government ministers are then faced with a problem. They can't afford to be saying "What a great curriculum - shame about the teachers." For the NC to have any effect, rather than just look pretty, it must be teachers who make it work. And if all the teachers are misguided or incompetent, then you need to replace them all. In the current climate that would be very difficult indeed. So there is occasional soft-pedalling, where tribute is paid to the hard work teachers do, or it is emphasised that the misguided ones, the ones who fell for the silly left-wing theories, are only a small minority. (In which case, you might think, they hardly matter.)

We cannot get a clear view of teachers from ministerial pronouncements, and that there should be some inconsistency is understandable. Teachers are not a unified homogeneous group, any more than pupils, parents or secretaries of state. There are good ones and bad ones, keen ones and lazy ones, traditional and progressive ones, and vast numbers in between. But we do need a clear view of teachers in the National Curriculum, because unless their role has been clearly identified there is little chance of the whole business working.

HMI did try to advise on this point, in a report to Kenneth Baker. "Too many teachers feel their profession and its work are misjudged and seriously undervalued, " they wrote. There will be a significant improvement only when teachers -
"are sufficient in number, suitably qualified and experienced, and so committed to the changes that, unsupervised, in thousands of classrooms, they will bring their professional skills and competence to bear upon the job."

That "unsupervised" is crucial. There is no practical way of policing the education profession if large numbers of teachers are hostile to what is proposed; regardless of doctrine, it has to be something which the teachers can deliver, and that ought to be taken into account when the 'something' is being defined. That is the challenge, but the only Education minister to take it seriously was John

MacGregor.

"From Policy to Practice" virtually outlines a curriculum without teachers. They are one of the key audiences for the document, in that it will tell them what to do and when to report, but they have little part in its definition (and in fact are seldom mentioned, with any active role).

## FREEDOM TO WORK

"What is specified will allow teachers considerable freedom in the way in which they teach, examples and materials used, selection of content, use of textbooks, etc." (4.15)

They may say it. They may even mean it. But that is not the experience of many teachers. Many of them find they are having to cover more subject matter than ever before, and as a result they have less choice about how to tackle topics, and less chance of varying their approach so as to improve the quality of learning. Their freedom to operate as they wish, to control and plan their own work, has been diminished.

A history teacher is part of a group which meets to plan resources for teaching the National Curriculum to eleven year-olds. They want pupils to understand the reasons for the collapse of the Roman Empire. These reasons are complex, and involve absorbing a range of information from different sources. The group prepares attractive materials, at least nine separate pieces of writing for pupils to read and understand.

Now, what should the task be ? It might be the traditional essay, but it might also be television documentaries. This teacher, like Mr. Clarke, knows that not all work is easy. But she also knows that there is no virtue in making it dull, and that by providing a purpose and audience for the work she may get a more active involvement on the part of pupils, and a deeper understanding.

What she proposes to do is set up small groups to prepare short TV documentaries. Each group works on a different aspect of the material, so that when they come to perform their items they can learn both as performers and as audience. The items may actually be filmed and kept for later use, or could simply be performed live. Then different groups might be formed, containing a mixture of the documentary groups, who can then pool their knowledge towards a newspaper account of the downfall of the Roman Empire, selecting evidence from what they have heard and read.

That is an ambitious and interesting assignment, which many pupils would enjoy but also learn from. The snag is, when the teacher looks at her programme she has two double lessons for the whole thing. There is so much other material that she cannot do what she wants - and what she thinks her pupils need. She can tell them all the conclusions herself and hope that something will sink in, or she can keep to her proposed assignment and risk leaving out parts of the curriculum which the law requires her to cover. What she cannot do is a decent, satisfying job.

"From Policy to Practice" did envisage a role for teachers in the necessary revision of National Curriculum:"The experiences of teachers and their professional advice will give essential indications, right from the outset, of the need for and nature of changes." (5.2)

It hasn't happened. Teachers have many complaints about the NC, but their main one would probably be the refusal to value their opinion. Some changes have been made, but few in proportion to the catalogue of insensitive and inept decisions. Not only are our experiences discounted, they are often directly ridiculed.

"I wasn't wildly impressed with the criticism from the particular interest groups."
(Kenneth Clarke, commenting on reactions to his proposals for History and Geography, Feb. 91)

A further complaint is the place of teachers in the assessment process. The initial decision to split NCC and SEAC identified assessment as a crucial political area, in some way separable from the business of teaching, and this dangerous separation has persisted through the ensuing arguments - with the recurrent insistence from Government that where external tests collide with teacher judgements then it will be the external tests which prevail.

Teacher judgements are not perfect, and it was a regular and worrying finding of HMI that some teachers had low expectations of their pupils. So it is reasonable, for teachers as well as for the public, to look for some evidence in addition to teacher assessment. Kenneth Clarke, however, sees this not as a collaboration but as a battle:
"A quite extraordinary proportion of British teachers have been raised in

a culture which is quite hostile to organised testing of any kind apart from their own."

I see it rather differently. With many teachers there is a nervousness about assessment, a recognition that their opinion of a child's performance may differ from someone else's, which is entirely understandable. It is, indeed, a condition of our fallible human judgement ("that it can be set right when it is wrong" as Mill puts it), but that does not mean we are blase about the whole process. The tension with which exam results are collected, the energy which goes into moderation, the interest in reading scores, the hours of unpaid effort devoted to marking - all these testify that teachers take assessment seriously, and wish it to improve.

We do not take kindly, though, to being patronised. A SEAC leaflet ("Teacher Assessment at Keystage 3", issued in Dec. '91) expensively informed us that:

Teacher assessment is part of everyday teaching
Teachers exercise their own professional judgement
Pupils can be actively involved in assessment
Records can help in planning future work
Evidence is needed to support judgements
Good reports help parents to understand their children's work in school.

All this we knew, and none of it has anything specific to do with the National Curriculum. Teacher assessment, the leaflet sagely concedes, " is not something new. It has always been an essential part of teaching and learning."

So, what is new ?

"What is new is a national structure of assessment objectives - the statements of attainment in the NC. Also new is a common reporting structure - the NC ten level scale."

Yes, those are new. But do they help ? How or why do they improve the assessment which has already been taking place ? That simple, crucial question is not answered; instead we get the promise of further glossy publications, and a series of conferences. These are not to explore the issues, or to raise questions, but "to consider arrangements for the tests."

That is what makes teachers angry, the assumption that they have to be taught how to suck eggs because nobody has played this game before. It is hard to convince outsiders that this is a serious problem. There used to be teachers' strikes; now it's all gone quiet. Everyone who appears in public seems to be in favour of the National Curriculum - surely the teachers are, too ?

Some of them may be. Many of them are in favour of the idea - the value of an agreed framework, which relates work across the country, and across the junior-secondary divide. But the peculiar fashion in which this National Curriculum has been implemented leaves a bitter taste in the mouths of many teachers, and the fact that that bitterness has not been reported publicly is a further irritation. Just because we're not on the news doesn't mean that we're happy.

This bitterness is accentuated by political impotence. We don't have negotiating rights, the government can legislate on a whim without consultation, and the atmosphere of public discussion is reluctant to take us seriously. There is an air of revenge - "They thought they were special, so they had it coming" - and a relish in the way media commentators dismiss signs of teacher unrest.

The signs are there. In levels of stress, in the numbers of good people who give up teaching before retirement age, and in the frightening statistic that two thirds of young teachers leave the profession within their first five years. And at the other end, I am weary of going to retirement parties where good teachers are so obviously relieved to be giving up work. Maybe it's our fault, maybe we deserve it, but we are not happy.

CAUSES FOR CONCERN

The reasons are various, and some of them go back for years. There are additional factors, however, related to the introduction of NC, which have made the situation worse. I believe that the most powerful frustration for teachers is not low pay but the lack of control over their own work, and here the NC has severely restricted our chances of job satisfaction. In the previous chapter, I suggested that the massive definition of the NC could be a disincentive for bright pupils, in seeming to devalue the originality of their future work - "It's all been done. We know what learning is; look in the folder."

If that is true for pupils, it is even more true for teachers. To read most of the NC literature, we are not professionals, but postmen "delivering" packages which someone has defined as worthy of receipt by all our pupils. There are token phrases about us using our judgement, and the NC leaving us free to choose our method, but if the size of the syllabus and the method of assessment are chosen for us, then that freedom rapidly begins to shrink.

This is not an argument for anarchy. Many teachers are in favour of some form of national curriculum, and would echo criticisms that our traditional arrangements have been haphazard. They want to be accountable, and are prepared to accept the discipline and constraints which that involves - just as talented individual teachers thrive on their membership of department teams, which make demands on them, but also leave them room for the exercise of creativity and individual judgement. What is important is not to defend barricades marked ORDER or FREEDOM, but to look for an intelligent combination of the two.

This danger was most poignantly expressed by Mrs. Thatcher. In an interview, she expressed fears that the National Curriculum framework had become too prescriptive:
"When we first started on this, I do not think we ever thought they would do the syllabus in such detail. And I always felt that when we had done the core curriculum, the core syllabus, there must always be scope for each teacher to use her own methods, her own experience.

So I did not really feel that the core curriculum or any subject should take up all the time devoted to that subject because otherwise you are going to lose the enthusiasm and the devotion of all the extras that a really good teacher can give out of her own experience."

This is ironic, in the sense that it is hard to conceive of any National Curriculum passing into law without Mrs. Thatcher's supportive glare around the Cabinet table, but she is right. People in responsible jobs need to feel free to make decisions if they are going to make the fullest use of their talents, and many teachers feel that National Curriculum has severely limited that freedom.

Kenneth Clarke argues that teachers should gain increased job-satisfaction
"once they see themselves knowing what they are expected to deliver, knowing that what they're delivering is what the public now expects."

This is not the way it looks to 'Alan Bell', a history teacher: .

"The people who are formulating these ideas are blind. They are leading us - but they want us to go in front of them along the awkward path towards the precipice. I feel that everything I have done in the past has been better from an educational view than what I may do in the future. And that's the kind of thing that makes you ask yourself 'Shall I carry on ?'."(from an article in The Guardian 13.3.90).

This is Lesley Chandler, head of a junior school in Lewisham:
"The National Curriculum is to be in place in September for five-year-olds. We thought the consultation documents would be pretty much the shape of the final papers, given that they came out fairly recently and with a consultation period so truncated that no-one seriously believed we were being asked for our considered opinions.

But no, sections of the Science document have disappeared. And though it is rumoured that copies of the final documents have been sighted, word is that they can only be secured by writing to York from a home address. They have yet to arrive in the staff rooms. The contempt of this Government for professionals has to be experienced to be believed."

Following a study of teacher turnover in 1989, Professor Alan Smithers concluded that "Teachers have been unsettled by so many changes of direction from the Government and have a sense of not being valued as a profession. Many teachers who would have seen the job through to retirement are taking up the offer of early retirement instead and these are senior people who would have formed the backbone of the profession in coming years."

In the three years since then, nothing has changed - except that the rate of change has increased, with an accompanying ferocity which makes it even harder to predict what will come next. The following examples (real people, with the names changed) indicate the various ways in which teachers come under pressure from the NC process.

Anne is a primary teacher, who came into teaching late but loves it. She runs a home and a classroom, and can just about manage both - until the folders start to arrive. Official documents, with legal backing, suggest to her that there is more work she should be doing, new demands to worry about. Implicitly, the effort she has been putting in till now is not enough, since nobody is suggesting what she should give up. She wants to do a good job, she hates the feeling of not being on top of the work, and the claims on her time are already excessive; so she does the rational thing - she stops teaching.

Bettina is a science teacher. In the early days, she went to meetings, where colleagues were roughly polarised between cynicism ("It'll never work") and the new realism ("That's the law; like it or not, that's what we've got to do."). She's not a cynic. Faced with the monumental task of assessing scientific skills under SAT 1 she made out a huge grid, displayed on the classroom wall, in which individual pupil names are matched against more than twenty statements of achievement. And that is for one class, for one attainment target, out of seventeen.

Then they change the rules. The seventeen targets don't apply any more. The grid comes off the wall. Her copy of the NC is covered with crossings out, where the regulations have been amended. Yes, the new demands are simpler, but what about the work and commitment which she has already put in, which now seems to be wasted ? Does she do it all again, and wait for the next set of revisions ? Or isn't there a temptation to slow down, to see what happens, rather than bust a gut for nothing ?

Chris is a head of department. He is quiet, intelligent and efficient, a leader who works through persuasion and example rather than bluster. Together he and the teachers in his department have worked out how they can assess the National Curriculum, maintaining the best of their current practice while also coping with the demands of the new paperwork. But they are operating a system which is being overhauled. They have to keep recording attainments for targets which no longer apply, and they are due to receive details of a "pencil-and-paper test", a simple exam which will instantly assess what their pupils have achieved in the last three years. They won't set the test; they'll just be told to mark it. Does Chris  pretend that this is the best way to assess pupils ? Does he lead a demonstration to Sanctuary Buildings ? Or does he just occasionally question whether the whole charade is worth it ?

Finally, a personal example. I teach an English group, year 9 as we call them now, and in the summer of '93 they will be among the first generation to be tested at the end of Keystage 3. Before the end of the summer term, with other members of the department, I decided which books I wanted to use. During the summer holidays I prepared an outline of what I wanted to teach.

In September I came back to school, and learned from my daily newspaper the titles of the three Shakespeare plays to be examined in the summer. Later in September I received from SEAC a thick, glossy ring-binder, containing an expensive 30-page leaflet. Two of these pages refer to English.

From them I learn that "it is likely that there will be four tiers" of tests, in which only the top two tiers will be tested on Shakespeare. (A direct contradiction of earlier promises that all pupils would be studying a Shakespeare play). As it happens, I teach a mixed-ability group for English, and this year's timetable has been constructed on that premise. If the Government was requiring streaming throughout the land then we would need to be told that in May.

There are a few other points where I could do with more clarification: "Precise details of the tiers and the numbers and lengths of papers" will be issued in October. "A suggested reading list designed to support general teacher assessment of reading throughout the key stage will be sent to schools in November." I will get an anthology of literary and non-literary material, as a basis for a reading test, but not until February. There will be some sample test items for reading tests in the lowest tier, but they will arrive in November, the same month that I shall be sent guidance for the choice of prose fiction, poetry and drama I may wish to cover. And if I'm impatient for "more information on the tests themselves, including examples of test items, mark schemes and pupils' responses" they're also available - but not until November. Why not just say they're not ready, and postpone everything until they are ?

The National Curriculum is not a total disaster. There are teachers of Technology who have been cheered by the recognition it gives them, teachers of English who recognise creative possibilities in the programmes of study, and teachers at all levels who welcome any attempt to establish continuity across the junior-secondary divide. Many primary teachers welcomed the attempt to bring greater breadth and more rigorous thought to the planning of their work. The impact varies from teacher to teacher, and subject to subject. A secondary teacher of Science or Maths may feel shell-shocked by the paperwork and revisions, but at least they have a place, and some sort of job security. An Art teacher, originally promised core status with all pupils up to 16, is now back to the optional fringe, and a very uncertain pattern of assessment. Do you want to be part of the ten levels game, or would you rather be left alone ? Or would you prefer to work in a primary school, attempting to master not one NC document but six - with another three to come ?

But it's bitty. There isn't the sense that this is a successful operation, working in favour of the kids. With GCSE there were twenty years of development work, lots of staff room arguments about standards, exams, levels and evidence, but as the shape became clearer so many teachers could feel the benefit, could justify the marking and moderation time to themselves, because it was a system that worked. I don't have that confidence about the National Curriculum, and I don't know anybody else who does either.

There is a fair bit of public whistling, assuming that anything with this much public approval and government money must work out all right in the end - despite evidence to the contrary. Many people want it to work, and there are strong pressures against saying too loudly that it's not working, so perhaps if we all stay quiet and keep our heads down it may turn out OK.

I doubt it. I think working in education commits us to hypothesis and argument, to testing assumptions and examining the evidence. From what I see and know, the current NC arrangements will not bring us quality education, and if that is true, then we had better say so as quickly as possible.

QUALITY

What are the features of good work ? You can read a lot of NC documents, including many statements of attainment, without meeting an attempt at a definition of quality. Some would say "You know it when you see it," but I think we can do better than that.

Pupils benefit from attractive surroundings and decent materials. They work better when they are clear about the work they have been set, have some say in defining the task, and in evaluating their own performance. They respond to enthusiastic teaching, consistent standards and high expectations, with the regular encouragement of sensible praise. And such teaching is more likely under enlightened leadership, with clear priorities, rational working conditions and the support of professionals outside the school.

I haven't made this up. It's there, in lots of research and case studies, and educationists of very different persuasions would not dispute it. But it is light years away from the mumbo-jumbo of "Assuring Quality", which assumes that frequency of meetings between government appointed bodies, regularly reported on in glossy covers, will by itself achieve the miracle.

The kind of quality I describe is what teachers are after. Some of them are gloomy and many of them are worried, but when they're happy in their work it's because they have generated that kind of involvement, been part of a communal exploration which is creative - in Pottery, Science or PE, whether the kids are five or seventeen. That is what we are about, and I don't find any of it in the pages of the National Curriculum.

What do the advertising agencies do, when the government ask them to attract people into teaching ? They stress the excitement, the involvement, the personal contact. Will this boy grasp the idea ? Will that girl stop being so bored? If the rhetoric were true, adverts would be inviting students to "Come and teach the National Curriculum..join the national crusade and apply attainment targets "

It's ludicrous. Whatever draws young people into teaching, it won't be the National Curriculum. The NC brings instant guilt, by listing all the things you won't have time to do, the topics you'll skim superficially because there's no room to do them properly. The NC brings bitterness because its short, chaotic history already confirms what the staff room cynics asserted all along - they haven't thought it out, they don't mean it, there isn't any cash, it's just a bit of flannel for the voters. It's frustrating for the teachers, it's not a gain in quality - and it isn't even the best we can do.

No, what excites people is a sense of passion, a touch of soul, something with a dash of poetry:
"An artist, a poet, a radical pioneer, a stringent stimulating teacher, she had faith and character, her work in the school was an intimate echo of her inner life. She loved her fellow men, gave herself generously for others and by losing herself in her appointed task gained new life and power.
Nothing but the best she believed was good enough for children and she strove to surround them with beautiful things and create for them an environment that was charged with light. She believed that education was much more than success in examinations, though a long list of distinctions proved that the two were not incompatible.
She believed in the fundamental goodness of human nature, in liberty, in gentleness and in the silent but inevitable influence of cultivated surroundings. She was a high voltage cable in a progressive and cordial society."
(Sir Michael Sadler, describing a headteacher)

Mystical stuff. Part of a bygone age, you might think, where it was respectable to have dreams rather than profile components. You might get a nostalgic quiver down the spine, but you know it's an echo from another world. They don't make them like that any more. You would be wrong.

"It was a misty, murky morning, cobwebs standing out of the hedges. We stood still for five minutes just listening. Afterwards we wrote the sounds down, talked about them, and the children improvised. It was brilliant."

That was Hilary, a student teacher on practice at a primary school, offering hope for the future. And so does Sonia, who has discovered performance indicators that work:

"My mum often talks of a teacher she had when she was five. That's recognition as far as I'm concerned. I think children's opinion is the one that counts."

# CHAPTER NINE: Could Do Better

So, what's wrong with the National Curriculum ?
- It is a political, not an educational act
- It has too many aims, and no coherent vision
- It does not meet the declared purpose of serving industry
- It has not been freely discussed
- It is too dominated by subjects
- It is not properly balanced
- It has no overall curriculum plan
- It is not designed for all children
- It does not take small schools into account
- It has not been supported with appropriate resources
- It is subject to the personal whims of ministers
- It has been rapidly, fitfully created by various bodies
- It has too much content
- It is written in language that is vague and dull
- It imposes an unworkable scheme of assessment
- It leaves insufficient room for subsequent development.

That is a substantial list. Some of the elements are linked to each other, but if all those statements are true - if even half of them are true - then we have a considerable problem. What do we do about it ?

To raise the question indicates the size of the problem, and helps to explain why it has not been raised before. For the structure is so extensive, and has been so forcefully imposed, that it is hard to conceive of alternatives. The very idea of an alternative, indeed, has been suppressed. We have never been asked "What kind of National Curriculum do we want ?" We have been told that we have got it, and "The National Curriculum" thus appears to be the only available model, whereas it is possible to envisage a quite different National Curriculum.

Kenneth Clarke claimed that "The new consensus has emerged because the Government has now won the argument." But there is no consensus, and there has been no argument. Even discussion has been noticeably lacking, and that is one powerful reason for the mess we have. Again, John Stuart Mill saw it coming:
"Where there is a tacit convention that principles are not to be disputed;

where the discussion of the greatest questions which can occupy humanity is considered to be closed, we cannot hope to find that generally high scale of mental ability which has made some periods of history so remarkable."

## SECOND THOUGHTS

We do not have a real consensus between parties; we do not even have a consensus within the Conservative party. I have already mentioned Mrs. Thatcher's misgivings (p.102). A former Education minister, Sir Keith Joseph, also has reservations:

"..I wonder whether the national curriculum might not impose too tight a straitjacket...A national curriculum as tightly imposed as that may neglect non-academic children; it may impose, for non-academic children, a dilute academic curriculum..."

Stuart Sexton, a former key adviser, is also unhappy:

"Not only was the legislated national curriculum against all good Tory principles of the market, of devolved responsibility, of personal responsibility, of parental possibility, but it is being done very badly anyway."(4.7.92)

It is not only politicians who have misgivings. As the NC roundabout has gathered speed a series of educationists have either jumped off - or been pushed. I have already quoted the views of Professor Paul Black (chairman of TGAT, member of NCC) and Eric Bolton (Senior Chief Inspector, HMI). This is Peter Dines, former secretary of SEAC:

"As for the evaluation of the assessment arrangements, we at SEAC had set up a most thorough system which yielded results, about which the Government did not want to know, such as the unreliability of the so-called league tables. Sadly, this work was suppressed and the unit responsible is, I believe, being disbanded. This seems to me the greatest indictment of the present administration. They prefer prejudice to fact, dogma to research." (from a letter to "The Guardian" 29.8.92)

Duncan Graham, the first chief executive of NCC, also believes that things are going wrong:

"When Kenneth Clarke began to tell teachers how to teach, preferring his own gut prejudices to the evidence, the warning signs were clear. With advice now coming from 'tame' advisory councils and an emasculated schools inspectorate, the risks are obvious." ("The Observer", 6.9.92)

With this mounting chorus of disapproval, it is tempting to ask: who is actually in favour of this stuff? There's a lot of power behind it, and a ton of publicity, but which educational thinkers of repute consider that our National Curriculum is a positive and coherent framework for the future? Meanwhile, the roundabout roars on, loud and unquestioning, with a momentum of its own.

While you're on the roundabout, it all looks quite reasonable, and things only started to go wrong at the time you got off. From where I stand, it's been out of control for some time. Some would argue that while Government ministers have gone a little wild, the National Curriculum is fundamentally sound. At the moment, it's hard to separate the two, but National Curriculum will only look healthy, and have a chance of survival, when it is established as an independent structure, divorced from dogma.

Even within the citadel, all is not well. The NCC "Corporate Plan 1992 - 5" looks on the surface like business as usual - glossy cover, nine pages of useful text in a publication of sixteen pages. Compared with the quality of most teaching materials, it's lavish,and such profligacy has to be set against the laments about a budget reduced to 9.2 million pounds. Initially, the NCC self-confidence survives intact:

"This Corporate Plan redefines the role and priorities of Council in providing the Secretary of State with authoritative, timely and independent advice on all aspects of the curriculum..."

You can't help thinking that if that were right somebody else would be saying it. This is particularly true of the claim to independence; few outside observers would rate the NCC highly on this score, and it obviously worries them.

"Much will depend on the authority of NCC and the commitment of members and officers to the provision of high quality advice which is based on a responsive and independent stance."(p.9)

What they actually do is advise the Secretary of State on such matters "as he may refer to it or as it may see fit", "advise the Secretary of State on, and if so requested by him assist him to carry out programmes of research..." and "carry out such ancillary activities as the Secretary of State may direct." You don't have to be a genius to see who's in charge. There's a new stress on preparing pupils "for adult life", and a curious attempt to blend commercial and intellectual values:

"The National Curriculum will meet its objectives if teachers, parents, governors and employers believe in both the concept and the product." (p.9)

There is news, though, in the resolution that "Council intends to consult schools..." (p.3) about its future direction, and a promising agenda is laid out in the section on "Priorities":

"Council will consider - whether the problems which teachers are experiencing as they translate the NC Orders into practice are related to the nature of the Orders themselves, to teachers' own knowledge and understanding, to current models of curriculum organisation and classroom management, to other issues, or whether they are simply teething difficulties inevitable in a period of transition...

...Council will examine whether the weight of detail and the structure of programmes of study, attainment targets and statements of attainment should be rendered less complex and prescriptive....

...the curriculum should not be driven by assessment issues and NCC will work closely with SEAC to ensure that testing complements curriculum coherence..." (pp.4-5)

You can see the headlines now -
RETHINK ON CURRICULUM; TEACHERS OVERLOADED;
TESTING DISTORTS LESSONS, SAY NCC CHIEFS.

But you didn't see them then (December 1991), because these weren't 7 year old reading scores or GCSE grades under fire. Given the lack of an independent, critical press, this change of direction doesn't make the news.

NCC and SEAC are now to be merged, and only time will tell if this kind of reflection will be allowed to take effect; the independence of the NCC is very much in doubt, and what we sceptics need is not assertions of integrity, but instances of the NCC expressing an opinion contrary to that of the Secretary of State. We shall see.

They have a different dream. Tucked away in a section headed "Enabling Mechanisms" we find the usual boring, self-important terminology - "Informing Council", "Advising on Implementation" but then an unaccustomed flash of imagery lightens up the gloom:
- "Winning hearts and minds."

The brief fling with consultation is over as they return to their first love, going steady with evangelism, pushing the product. I'm not sure it's wise to suggest parallels with the Vietnam war, that expensive, destructive and prolonged attempt by an alien power to impose their patterns of thought on the resident population, but maybe they know best.

It is probably good news that the Chairman of the NCC is prepared to look at revising the NC for primary schools. The way he describes the process, though, is not hopeful:
"Now that the complete framework is in place, NCC is in a position to ask whether this is the right curriculum and whether it is working as we would all wish."

First assemble the machinery, then carry out the fine tuning. But "the complete framework" is massive and unwieldy, and it has been assembled with no concern for what "we" would all wish. He says, very reasonably, that "Radical change can only succeed with the support, commitment and ownership of those most affected"; he does not say that to date the whole NC process has operated in defiance of that principle.

It is no exaggeration to say that the nature of the education system, and the pattern of the national curriculum, has changed with each secretary of state. This is a ludicrous state of affairs for teachers, who cannot with confidence plan beyond a very immediate future.

We have a curious paradox, of a government mad for testing which is working on untested hypotheses. Assumptions are made, acted on and turned into law without anyone bothering to find out if they are true. Is spelling the most important kind of mistake ? Is coursework an unreliable form of assessment ? Are privatised, amateur inspectors necessarily more efficient than trained professionals? We don't know, and nor do they, but they have the power to legislate.

This brand of education has no energy or enthusiasm about it; it's a dour imposition of received wisdom, with no room for questioning or innovation. And curiously, for something that so prides itself on quality and standards, it isn't actually very clever or clear. It doesn't matter how many O levels John Major got; it does matter that his cabinet are eager to prescribe the pattern of an education service to which they are not prepared to entrust their own children. This is education for other people's kids, medicine that will do them good.

Shakespeare, for instance. Now, why should Kenneth Clarke be so proud of his ability to ensure that everyone studies Shakespeare (even if his successor dilutes this claim) ? Is it because he has enjoyed the plays, or learnt political wisdom from them ? Will Keystage 3 pupils have learnt about interaction between characters, a more responsive understanding of other points of view ? Or does the study of Shakespeare lead to a more sensitive awareness of language, the excitement of imagery ?

Not if we're to judge by Kenneth Clarke:
"Grant maintained schools are now an established part of the landscape. We will not rest on our laurels. As grant maintained schools break the mould of the old discredited ideas, this first hundred must be seen as only the beginning of sweeping reform." (The Guardian 17.7.92).

You can hear the crash of mixed metaphors, the yawn as the cliches accumulate. You can see the distance stretching, between the weary word-pictures, and the facts of the situation they purport to describe: that a few schools have got a lot of money, which has been spent on management salaries and carpets.

Kenneth Clarke doesn't have to be a poet. But he shouldn't write like this and then presume to dictate which writings should be studied in school, overruling people whose business it is to know about writing. The main charge is arrogance, and while this may sound like a moral quibble, it is having very practical results. We are in the process of damaging our children's education.
My anger is shared, across a wide range of political opinion. Despite the caricatures, teachers are not loony radicals; most are conservative, and many are Conservative, explicitly sharing the public concern to raise standards in education, wanting to be part of a growth in quality.

The National Curriculum has given them few opportunities for such involvement. Not only have there been false starts and damaging revisions, but the advent of NC has actually prevented positive developments elsewhere. In GCSE, Records of Achievement, Appraisal and Cross-curricular Issues, many teachers saw a programme for positive improvement. Yet work in all these areas has been distorted or delayed by the prior demands of National Curriculum.

It is hard to get the balance right. There is, in the energy of pupils and the commitment of teachers, a resilience which can survive political lunacy, doing good work despite the odds and the hostile rhetoric. On the other hand, many chances have been wasted, much money misspent, good teachers have been lost and some irrevocable decisions made. We have to do more than simply soldier on.

Part of our frustration stems from our inability to do more than tinker with the details. HMI are being privatised, and local authorities - who in many cases perform a valuable co-ordinating role - are also under attack, seeing their resources dwindle by the month. Having abrogated so much of the power, it is only government which can make a substantial difference, and government has shown itself very reluctant to listen, let alone to make lasting revisions.

A BETTER WAY ?

I am not going to offer an alternative blueprint, a personal version of the National Curriculum which I would like imposed tomorrow. That, too, would be arrogant. But I do think it is possible to outline some of the features of an improved system, and it is vital that we consider some alternatives: already government ministers defend the mess we have on the grounds that "It's better than the mess we used to have - do you want to go back ?"

We don't. We want to go forward, to a pattern of education which has the confident support of most people. It is very likely that such a pattern will include some kind of national curriculum, although I doubt whether that should be - or can be - the current version. But we do need something planned and permanent, and that means some form of consensus.

Mrs. Thatcher despised consensus as "the absence of principle and the presence of expediency." As an abstract idea, or a call to battle, that's quite attractive. As a practical programme it is a disaster. One of the reasons for spelling out recent mistakes and contradictions in such detail has been to demonstrate that "conviction politics" is not as simple as it sounds; it does not cut through problems as incisively as the rhetoric suggests.

John Stuart Mill, yet again, is relevant :
"Truth, in the great practical concerns of life, is so much a question of the reconciling and combining of opposites, that very few have minds sufficiently capacious and impartial to make the adjustment with an approach to correctness, and it has to be made by the rough process of a struggle between combatants fighting under hostile banners."

We need, not simply conviction, but debate. Genuine exchange, leading to some form of consensus, however limited. It is easy to despise consensus, but only some form of agreement, across political parties and beyond them, will give us the kind of long-term stability which English education so desperately requires.

Teachers need to prepare for something which has a reasonable chance of being there in five years' time, let alone ten. There has to be some kind of consultation, if only to avoid the cost of ignorance, and that means creating a body which can speak for the teaching profession. In the past teacher unions have talked of it, and even government ministers have toyed with the idea, but the need is urgent now.

Education needs political support; it needs to be taken seriously and constructively discussed, to be given the resources its importance deserves. But it does not need the petty infighting, casual slurs and impulsive decision-making to which we have become accustomed over the past five years.

If the National Curriculum is to be defined in terms of content, that content has to be less. There might be a distinction between "what has to be done" and "what might be done", but if we are serious about public involvement in discussion then it ought to be possible to put the minimum content requirements of each subject on one sheet of paper, written in language most people can understand. That might scare some subject specialists, but it would guarantee that a wider range of people could become involved in the debate.

Early in this debate, government ministers took delight in disparaging English education by comparison with other systems in Europe. They might now usefully look at how it is that successful rivals can produce a national curriculum that can be contained within a single pamphlet. We should be so lucky.

There would need to be other pieces of paper defining the overall pattern of the curriculum, indicating what importance was being placed on particular subjects, and why. The record of revision over the past four years suggests that it would be hard to reach agreement on a substantial core. Personally, I think this is is a pity, but it is a tough political choice which is either taken or not taken. I would rather have an honest admission that it cannot be taken, than a blast of trumpets announcing that it has been taken - followed by a series of retreats which render that announcement meaningless. Generally, we need thought before publicity, and legislation last of all.

Assessment is difficult, and it is the failure of education to get its act together on assessment which accounts for some of the present muddle. Parents and employers are not clear about assessment, and it is that vacuum of understanding which permitted the imposition of the ten-level pattern. That is understandable, but it is far from being the best we can do.

The detailed history of NC assessment is a record of factions at war. Government pronouncements and the deliberation of working groups alternate, swinging wildly between different patterns and styles, desperate to correct wrong impressions or appeal to particular lobbies. This is no way to tackle a complex problem. There has to be careful, sustained thought, over a period of time, involving people with expertise. It may involve others as well, and it will certainly attract criticism and debate. But the current craze for instant solutions is not going to give us anything of lasting value, or reassure teachers that they are involved in something which will benefit their pupils.

There has to be consistency over resources. If we're serious about a National Curriculum, it will cost money. Choosing particular options because they are cheap is an indication that this is window-dressing rather than lasting reform. If assessment requires group moderation and a long-term commitment to trial marking, that is what it costs. Rushing to "pencil-and-paper tests" because the outlay is less will be very expensive in the long run - in the quality of lessons, the motivation of pupils, and the morale of teachers, who will know that their pupils are getting second best.

Above all, we need a commitment to the system. Over the past few years I have, like many teachers, faced an insidious thought. Perhaps this whole charade is not even meant to work ? Perhaps the aim is the disruption of state education, the better to boost the market. The more parents are encouraged to 'go private', the less will be the concern for quality in comprehensive schools. Maybe we have a conspiracy here, dressed up in the rhetoric of improvement, to do damage and save cash.

I don't want to believe this. I don't honestly think it is as simple as that, and if it were it would leave us with grim alternatives - revolution or despair. So I believe the rhetoric, and carry on working and thinking, in the hope that we really are engaged in giving our children a better deal. But if we are, that needs to be an inclusive, universal provision, rather than an obsessive concern with separation - CTCs, assisted places, opting out. If the energy goes on helping people get out of the system, then the system is devalued - whatever the speeches say.

There would be an additional benefit from this. If we had a real commitment to the system, to spending time, thought and money on educating the whole population, then that would in itself provide an incentive to teach. Current cliche suggests that nobody now cares about ideals, that only money and individual greed act as incentives. I see those forces at work, in the young people I teach as well as in my colleagues, but I also see a strong sense of justice, an appeal to fundamental decency which rests on the assumption of equality - "That's not right, is it, sir ?"

I think that could bring recruits into an education system which was genuinely for all. Part of the current government case is that during the sixties a lot of sloppy ideas came into teaching, from which we've suffered ever since. I came into teaching in the sixties, but that's not my lasting memory.

What I remember is not the media obsession with flower power and drugs, but a new sense of possibility about what schools might be like - and a sense of companionship with the large number of people who entered teaching at the same time. We may have been naive, there may have been inadequacies in our training, and we certainly had more access to resources than we do now, but we were part of something exciting, and that excitement came from the fact that this was education for all - not for the rich, or the boys, or the bright, but for all. That was the comprehensive ideal.

Times have changed. There is less money about, we are more hard-headed, and in many ways teaching is far more sophisticated and effective than it was then. We do, after all, learn as we go along. But I think we would all benefit, and we would also recruit more and better teachers, if we could recapture that sense of purpose, that belief that all children are entitled to a education of quality.

The first step is to value the state system that we have, to remind people of what it can do, and to show people in it and outside it that the work within it matters. It was a Conservative Education Minister, Edward Boyle, who provides the best model for this. Part of his contribution was political, making decisions and arguing in cabinet for resources; but a massive part of it was personal - expressed in visits to hundreds of schools. He took the politician's most precious currency - time - and spent it on the system, taking people seriously, looking at what was going on before opening his mouth, and then speaking in a tone which was positive, encouraging, enthusiastic.

It would be nice to see an Education Minister who took Boyle as their model. We have become used to a situation where the police and the armed forces have particular politicians who speak up on their behalf, who protect their pay and remind the public of the contribution they make, but nobody speaks for teachers. The votes, apparently, are all the other way, so the fashion is for sneers and insults.

That would help to transform the climate outside, but we also need to protect the climate of the school. The first priority is to defend the educational work of schools, which may sound strange, but not to teachers. Local management was intended to make schools responsible for their resources, even to 'free' them in some sense, and for some (a favoured few, at the top end of the market) that may have happened. But even the winners report acquisition, expenditure and increased salaries - not innovations in learning. What we have all experienced, though, is the subversion of agendas, where meetings of teachers now discuss budgets, check through financial returns and calculate the necessary cuts.

Time that should go on education, and how that can be improved, is spent on balancing the books, or explaining staffing costs to the governors. It has become difficult for school managements to focus on their main job - how children are learning - and that may help to explain why more heads retire early, and why senior staff get so far up the ladder and then choose not to proceed. If we are going to get quality education, we have to find ways of managing that, beyond paying bonuses to management.

We certainly need more sophisticated models of success. The current government view is fiercely competitive - the good teacher is the one who, ahead of others, wins incentives and rewards; the good school is the one that dominates the market, wins more than its share of pupils, resources and good staff. If the aim is good education for one pupil, or for a few, those models are sufficient. If, on the other hand, we are talking about a successful system, then the models must be different. A good teacher might be one that helps others become better; a good school could be an example of successful practice, which through openness makes its insights available to other schools. This kind of sharing, specific local collaboration, can work and has worked well, through consortia, primary-secondary links, the process of GCSE moderation.

In ILEA, ironically, the serious work had actually begun: the use of exam results to identify differences between schools, and to focus on under-achievement; the specific analysis of the role of management in supporting learning, and the subsequent need both to identify good practice, and to direct the staff development of those members of school management who required it. These were difficult but necessary aims, but the tragedy is that at the precise moment when the best local authorities have been developing such work, central government has decreed their failure.

Nobody's perfect. The best teachers, confident as they are, talk about what they are doing with colleagues, gain from watching and listening to each other, and use the responses of their pupils to check if their own subjective impressions are correct. Head teachers carry a heavy responsibility, but the ones who carry it alone have nervous breakdowns; the best heads listen - to governors and parents, LEA advisers, deputies and other staff, because only these people can tell them the things they do not know. And in the same way, government ministers have to acknowledge the experience of others - not as a ploy to earn sympathy or votes - but as a rational tactic, the best way to do business.

And this is where Mill comes in. His quiet, common sense has been at the heart of so many of our traditions that we have come to take him for granted, a kind of liberal platitude. But he reminds us now of truths that we desperately need: we listen to others, not just to be polite or make them feel good, but because only in that way can we think clearly ourselves. Liberty is not just good manners; it is a necessary condition of clear judgement.

The alternative, as we have painfully been taught, is arrogance:
"Unfortunately for the good sense of mankind, the fact of their fallibility is far from carrying the weight in their practical judgement, which is always allowed to it in theory; for while everyone knows himself to be fallible, few think it necessary to take any precautions against their own fallibility, or admit the supposition that any opinion, of which they feel very certain, may be one of the examples of the error to which they acknowledge themselves to be liable."

This is a familiar pattern, but it need not last for ever.

It was, amazingly, less than three years ago that a Tory Education Minister could say -
"I have taken the view that there was too heavy a burden on teachers. I always consult the troops before making a decision."

There are Conservatives who have been close enough to education - as councillors and governors, teachers and parents - to know that the recent pattern has been short-sighted and damaging, and that change - deliberate, controlled, intelligent change - is actually in the best interests of our children.

The present NC may seem like an immovable obstacle, but since it was enacted we have seen the removal of Mrs. Thatcher, the liberation of Eastern Europe and the crumbling of the Soviet Union. Monoliths are not for ever, especially if their foundations are weak. I think we have to look for improvement, maybe even radical reshaping. How on earth could this happen ?

There are a number of possibilities:

≈ a political change of mind, whereby it becomes expedient not to intervene in teaching matters quite so drastically or so often; votes in future elections might be won by a party which identified itself more realistically with support for education.

≈ more intelligent, constructive opposition. The Labour Party has found it expedient to echo Conservative criticisms, to accept that "Education is awful, but it's the Tories' fault". It is possible, as the Liberal Democrats showed in the 1992 election, to take a more constructive, genuinely critical stance, which commits politicians to a positive partnership with professionals. This did not win votes in 1992, but it might in the future.

≈ a clearer analysis in the media of what is going on, and how it might be changed. One of the ironies to me is that while "The Guardian" has supplied much of the information on which my analysis is based, its editorial stance towards the National Curriculum has for some time been uncritical, almost deferential. There are signs that this is starting to change. A considered television equivalent would be very welcome.

≈ some form of professional resistance. Commentators assume that "action" equals strikes, but there are alternatives. I personally would favour refusal to operate tests which have not been tested - prepared in advance, trialled, evaluated and then supplied to teachers before they embark on that course of study. It's not my decision, but there are other possibilities, and teachers will start to look at them.

≈ further defections from NC staff. It sounds like the Vichy government under Nazi occupation, but it must feel like that, too. If you're in there to make this work for the benefit of pupils, how do you feel when the latest government craze (traditional music teaching, attacks on English) are presented as your ideas ?

Many professionals have already defied the lunatic secrecy and crude bullying through which the NC is defined - but there must be more to come. Their working conditions, however plush, are morally intolerable.

≈ employers, as they incredulously grasp what is happening, will find ways of indicating to government that this kind of shambles does them no good at all. Replacing their sense of O level with ten different levels is only the start, but they will surely dispel the illusion that all this will somehow render our economy more competitive.

≈ parents finding their voice. Education has been absorbed into Chartermania, that festive glorification of the consumer. Logically, these consumers will want to offer an opinion on the product, even if most of the consultation has been one-way. (We are told that a referendum on the Maastricht treaty has been discounted partly on the grounds of cost, that it would be too expensive to send each household a summary. How many millions have been wasted on NC booklets for parents ?)

≈ seeing what happens. This is the worst scenario of all. The rhetoric has promised progress through simple stages, clearly tested at every stage, with the publication of results. How can this possibly be a success ?
The habit of denigration has become deeply ingrained, and tabloid newspapers simply would not know how to report educational success. The 1992 GCSE results show that simply getting good scores is not enough - good scores mean shoddy criteria, tests that aren't tough enough.
At some point, somebody is going to ask if the NC works, and when the results are seen to be complex and varied somebody else will say the whole thing has failed. There will be no independent expertise to consult, but it's a safe bet that teachers will be blamed.

It's that possibility that has to be born in mind when we talk about changing the National Curriculum. At some point there is going to be a row; it's just a question of deciding when, and on what terms. In my view, it's better for us to say honestly now that this charade will not work, rather than waiting for someone outside education to expose it.

Many teachers will feel they have suffered enough, but the simple passage of time will not cure the weaknesses identified in this analysis. There is, too, a difference between accepting necessary responsibility and suffering from the incompetent impositions of others. Given a positive role, and some stake in the improvement of our system, I think many teachers would be happy to work for a more creative, more sensitive pattern, which would give us the strength of a framework while still allowing the necessary freedom to innovate, develop and create.

How much of the National Curriculum would remain intact ? Which of the various bodies would continue to exist, and how would they be staffed ? How much more change from above can this battered system sustain ? It is not easy to say, and I find it hard to be sanguine about what comes next.

But for us to work at all, we have to maintain some faith, and mine is that we can do better. The idea of a National Curriculum is a good one, but the manner in which our current model has been imposed, and many of its particular features, mean that it will not bring the benefits which have so often and so confidently been promised. If that is, sadly, true, then we have to say so, not just in staff rooms but in newspapers and television programmes, so that employers, parents and pupils understand more about what is going on.

Knowledge is better than ignorance, discussion wiser than fear. We talk to each other, and go forward, rather than looking back and saying nothing. These are the choices education has taught us to make, and to keep faith with them and with the prospects of our children, we have to think, work and fight for a better future.

# INDEX

Labour Party
*41, 121*
Languages
*34, 44-5, 47*
Lawlor, Sheila
*23, 78*
Liberal Democrat Party
*41, 121*
MacGregor, John
*13-14, 45, 61, 62, 97-8, 120*
Major, John
*67, 78*
Market, the
*40-2, 83*
Maths
*31, 32, 35, 63, 68-9, 87, 89*
Mill, John Stuart
*7, 10, 15, 20, 29, 57*
*75, 100, 109-110, 115, 120*
Money
*28, 65, 76, 117, 118*
Murdoch, Iris
*18*
Music
*35, 46, 54-5, 63, 80*
NC publications
*32, 36, 58-60, 62, 65, 111-3*
NCC
*7, 45, 53, 55, 62, 99, 111-3*
Norwood, Report
*39*
Nursery Education
*42, 50*
Panorama
*17-18*
Parents
*8, 83-4, 89-94, 122*
Patten, John
*5-6, 8, 9, 29, 53*
PE
*35, 36, 45-6, 63, 80, 86*
Plato
*39, 56*

Primary schools
*28, 31-2, 35, 61, 103, 105, 108*
PSE
*33, 54*
Pupils
*74, 83, 85-9, 92-3, 106*
Quality
*5, 8, 58, 60-1, 83, 106-8*
Reading Recovery
*28-9, 65*
Resources
*64-5*
Richmond
*22-5*
ROA
*85-6*
Romans, the
*30, 98*
Rumbold, Angela
*17*
Science
*35, 37, 43-4, 46, 56, 59, 63, 72-3, 92, 104*
Scruton, Roger
*18*
SEAC
*14-5, 26-7, 54, 55, 56, 59-60, 62, 76, 77, 99*
Secondary Schools
*29, 31, 32*
Selection
*39-43, 48*
Sexton, Stuart
*78, 110*
Shakespeare
*48, 104, 114*
Shorrocks, Diane
*27*
Statemented pupils
*46*
Spelling
*5-6, 49, 66, 68-70, 92*
Straw, Jack
*19*